Third Edition

WOMEN RAINMAKERS'

BEST

MARKETING TIPS

Theda C. Snyder

ABA **LawPracticeManagementSection**
MARKETING • MANAGEMENT • TECHNOLOGY • FINANCE

Commitment to Quality: The Law Practice Management Section is committed to quality in our publications. Our authors are experienced practitioners in their fields. Prior to publication, the contents of all our books are rigorously reviewed by experts to ensure the highest quality product and presentation. Because we are committed to serving our readers' needs, we welcome your feedback on how we can improve future editions of this book.

BLISS cartoon on page 90 is reprinted with permission. © Harry Bliss. Used with permission of Pippin Properties, Inc.

Cover design by Gail Patejunas. Interior book design by Catherine Zaccarine.

Library of Congress Cataloging-in-Publication Data

Snyder, Theda C., 1948–
    Women rainmakers' best marketing tips / by Theda C. Snyder. — 3rd ed.
        p. cm.
    Rev. ed. of: Women rainmakers' best marketing tips / [edited by] Theda C. Snyder. 2nd ed. c2003.
    Includes indexes.
    ISBN 978-1-61632-024-9
    1. Women lawyers—United States—Marketing. I. Women rainmakers' best marketing tips. II. Title.
    KF316.5.W666   2010
    340.068′8—dc22

                                                                                    2010029987

12 11 10 5 4 3 2 1

Discounts are available for books ordered in bulk. Special consideration is given to state bars, CLE programs, and other bar-related organizations. Inquire at Book Publishing, American Bar Association, 321 N. Clark Street, Chicago, Illinois 60654.

Contents

Introduction

This book marks the twentieth anniversary of Women Rainmakers, a group formed in recognition of a simple truth: every lawyer needs to market. ABA Women Rainmakers is a unique group within the American Bar Association Law Practice Management Section. The LPM Section recognizes technology, management, finance, and marketing as four prongs of successful law practice management.

Successful lawyers recognize that they are selling every day—themselves, their skills, their points of view. A lawyer's book of business represents freedom: the freedom to manage one's own practice, the freedom bestowed by financial security, the freedom to leave one's current situation for another. Partners are expected to maintain a book of business, or they may be asked to leave. Associates will climb the law firm ladder faster if they can demonstrate an ability to be self-supporting. Even in-house, public interest, and government lawyers must market within their organizations.

Two themes emerged in writing this third edition of *Women Rainmakers' Best Marketing Tips*. The first is *appropriateness*. Appropriate marketing depends on many variables, including a wide range of characteristics of your target market as well as your own resources. The second is *search engine optimization (SEO)*. Any marketing outreach that relies on Internet distribution will be lost in the sea of electronic information unless it can rise to the top. Keywords, electronic descriptions, and metatags are the floatation devices of the Internet ocean, and marketers' language skills never have been more challenged.

The chapters retain many contributions and quotations from the original members of the Women Rainmakers Interest Group as well as the author's updates based on observations, research among today's rainmakers, and personal experience. Please note that a number of companies are mentioned in this book. Their inclusion is not an endorsement. Although modes of Internet communication continue to multiply, much remains the same. Rainmakers continue to rely on word of mouth, but the word is now transmitted electronically.

Internet technology has blurred the boundaries between different types of marketing techniques, because now the party providing content might also control the medium. Consequently, chapter headings are somewhat arbitrary; *e.g.*, the Websites material could as easily have been included in the public relations chapter as in the advertising chapter. Like boilerplate language in a contract, the headings do not control or limit the content of the chapter.

The information is offered on the RAM principle: Some suggestions may not be appropriate for you, and these you will *reject*. Others will fit your personal style, and these you will *accept*. Another group will not be exactly right, but the tips will work once you *modify* them.

Not every tip is appropriate for every lawyer. Indeed, some tips may be contradictory. Real contributions from real lawyers include the mistakes as well as the successes. By selectively using the RAM principle, you will find the techniques that create rain for your law practice.

Chapter 1

Your Marketing Plan

The most important issue in choosing your marketing tools is appropriateness. There are so many outlets for your message that choosing where to spend your time and money can be a difficult decision. Who is your target? Are you a BtoC (business to consumer) provider or a BtoB (business to business)? Whatever marketing tool you choose, make sure it is appropriate for you and for the recipient of the message.

Learn All You Can

If you feel that your marketing skills are lacking, take a few courses and read everything you can find on the subject. There is no lack of free information on the Web. Browse the local bookstore. Choose tools you're comfortable with and then use them—every day. Once you have a plan, the keys to carrying it out are preparation and determination. Keep your goal in mind and your expectations realistic. Above all, say women rainmakers, don't give up.

CHECK out some of the sites for sales professionals by searching "sales management blog." The best—and most jam-packed with useful information—may be Jeffrey Gitomer's Website, *www.gitomer.com*, and his books are worthwhile even though (because?) they have nothing to do with law.

TAKE marketing courses. I have taken courses on public relations sponsored by a weekly business magazine and a sales course given by a company that does mostly in-house courses for national sales staffs. I learned the nuts and bolts of how to prepare and issue press releases in the former. I learned important sales techniques to use in talking to clients in the latter. These included establishing preliminary rapport, overcoming objections, and handling complaints. In both places, I met new people, handed out cards, and made valuable business contacts.

HIRE a coach. Whether you're a sole practitioner, an associate trying to figure it out in a big firm, or somewhere in between, a weekly coaching session can help you define your goals and guide you in what you can do to achieve them. Some large organizations have arrangements with coaches. Check with your administration. Most coaches work over the phone, so it doesn't even matter where they are geographically. A coach doesn't tell you what to do; she helps you figure it out. Sometimes just having to articulate your thoughts to another person can lead you to the answer. A coach may be a superior choice if you have no one else to bounce ideas off of, you don't want to share marketing ideas with others who are essentially your competitors, or you want to be able to brainstorm ideas in a nonjudgmental setting.

If your firm doesn't have a coach allowance in its marketing budget, approach the marketing committee or managing partner about creating one.

BROWSE the marketing books in the business section of your local bookstore. Sometimes it's important to learn the marketing perspective of non-lawyers. You can adapt and shape the suggestions for your law practice.

CONSIDER bringing in a marketing consultant on a one-time basis to see where you are and to help you put together a plan. You can choose a small organization like LawBiz Management Company or turn to one of the big guys, such as Altman Weil or Hildebrandt, who mostly serve medium and large firms. A consultant is good choice if you need help getting and staying focused.

HELP in organizing your plan is a keystroke away. Type "marketing plan" into your search engine and start looking.

Market Research

Every plan should be based on market research. If that article in the morning paper prompted you to think about a new way to sell your legal services, you have just performed market research. Maybe you never thought of keeping abreast of new developments in the area in which you practice as market research, but it is. Consider, however, more targeted efforts. Market research encompasses many things: who needs your services, refining exactly what they need, how to reach that market, what motivates that target market, and who serves that market now.

O NE of the best ways to conduct market research is also the easiest. Be an omnivorous reader. The daily newspaper can be your most valuable information source. For example, when Orange County, California, filed the largest governmental bankruptcy proceeding in history, local practitioners often got their most current information from the daily mass media.

"First-mover advantage" describes the marketing head start gained by the first one ready to grab the affected market segment. Staying current on legal developments allows you to adjust your marketing plan quickly.

S ETTING up a Google Alert is easy and delivers content from both known and unknown sources to your inbox on the topics of your choice. Just enter the search term as you would for a Web search. I have gotten material from sources I would have never thought to search. When I commented on an article by a reporter on a city newspaper in another state, the response was, "How did you hear about this?" When you learn of a new development, figure out how it will affect your clients and make a plan to educate them about and satisfy that legal need.

L EXIS and Westlaw include electronic clipping services. Use one to keep track of your clients' activities. Explore different businesses on the Web, and subscribe to an industry electronic newsletter. Learn what's new with your clients—and their competitors—by periodically checking their Websites. You can discover needs for your services before your client even knows the needs exist, and clients are impressed that you take the time to learn the details of their work.

SUBSCRIBING to Websites and blogs in your practice area allows you to keep up, even if the news doesn't include one of your search terms. Look for a link to subscribe or a reference to RSS. ❘Subscribe to this blog's feed❘ The orange square with three white arcs is the symbol for RSS—Really Simple Syndication (formats that allow you to subscribe to frequently published material.) Copy and paste the URL of the site you want delivered into the "Add RSS" (or similar) box. You can also get a collection of pertinent news delivered to you by customizing iGoogle. If you have many subscriptions, rather than clutter your mailbox with all this incoming information, you can create a reader site to collect feeds from your favorite Websites and blogs. Examples are ***www.google.com/reader***, ***www.bloglines.com***, and ***www.my .yahoo.com***.

ONCE you learn to recognize them, you will realize that marketing research data are all around you. Look at your competitors' Web page or Yellow Pages advertisement. As you read slip opinions, pay attention to who represented the parties. You might undertake a Lexis or Westlaw search of cases in a given area to see if one firm dominates or if work is dispersed among many. Is there a referral opportunity? Are the firms breaking up or merging? Change at your competitor's shop can signal opportunity, as clients like stability, and they certainly don't like being asked to sign conflicts waivers.

IN many communities, legal gossip travels fast. Be prepared to act if you hear news that might open up a market for you. For example, let's say you have tried to get work from a large publicly

held company. Although you have excellent contacts among the in-house staff, the general counsel insists on sending all work to his ex-partner. Now you hear that the general counsel's contact is leaving the firm to accept a political position in Washington. Or maybe it's the general counsel who is leaving. Strike while the iron is hot! Call your contacts. Sometimes they are the last to know. Resend information about your firm. Make sure you are ready for consideration when the new broom sweeps clean.

WHEN a competitor sponsors a public seminar, consider attending. This allows you to check out what the competition is doing and perhaps meet other attendees. Report to your firm with a critique of what went well and what went badly. Use the information in fashioning your own marketing effort.

HOW many times have you received a phone call from a "shopper" client? This prospect asks for information about your ability to handle a case and your charges. Did you ever wonder if the would-be client is gathering information for one of your competitors? Many lawyers ask friends to gather information about a competitor so they can match *or beat* the competition's terms. Non-lawyer businesses do this all the time. How does your brochure and newsletter compare with others in the marketplace? You'll never know if you don't obtain a copy of others to see what's out there.

WHAT about price? Many lawyers will not divulge price information without a personal interview, but, depend-

ing on your area of practice, you may be able to learn a lot about how your competitors price their services. For example, are they billing hourly, or do they use alternative billing practices as a selling point?

Visit the business section of your local public library. Browse through the many directories of businesses. This may be available online through your library's Website. Some directories are limited to a specific industry. Some are arranged geographically. As you realize the breadth of the potential clientele, new marketing ideas are sure to pop into your head.

If you live near a tax-supported university, those libraries' resources are also available to you. Browse the periodicals in the business and law schools' libraries for marketing leads.

A directory or encyclopedia of associations can help you research organizations that would provide opportunities for writing, speaking, or exhibiting at a trade show.

Start collecting ideas from legal marketing experts by searching the Web. Search "marketing" on *www.abanet.org/lpm*. Check out "lawyer marketing" on *www.findlaw.com* and "client development" on *www.lexisone.com*. The Law Marketing Portal offers information at *www.lawmarketing.com*, and you can benefit from a unique viewpoint at the Association of Legal Administrators' site: *www.alanet.org*. The site for professional legal marketers is *www.legalmarketing.org*.

Find Your Niche

A market niche should be specific. Define your ideal client. Be specific as to the type of case this client will generate, case value, location, personal characteristics such as education or net worth, and referral potential. Once you can identify these characteristics, you can begin to define the best contact method.

Marketing to a niche includes figuring out the most appropriate way to reach that niche. Potential clients under thirty-five years of age seem most comfortable with electronic media. Older prospects may make more limited use of the Web and rely more on traditional print media, radio, and television. More ways to communicate seems to have made it harder, not easier, to make a personal connection. E-mail leaves the parties unable to picture the other or even hear their voice. Instead of attending a CLE (continuing legal education) seminar with an opportunity to network with other lawyers, you may earn that education credit by watching a Webinar at your desk. Your "end" may need to define the prospect by niche, which will in turn influence your choice of "means."

"You have to know your niche. For years there were clients who adored my work but would not send me cases. I had good rapport with our principal client's local office personnel. But the home office staff (all men) did not understand that when they had a 'bet the company' case, I was the one to handle it. Rather, they would send these cases to the senior partner, who in turn assigned them to me.

"I felt frustrated until I stopped to consider. My firm had had good relations with the client. We were getting all the business

they could send us. For me to compete with one of the men in my firm wasn't a good use of my time. I went back and reevaluated where I was getting my cases from and if I was shaking every bit of business out of those areas. When I did that, doors opened up, my life got much better, and things got much easier.

"Know who you are and where your business comes from. Also, recognize that there are some walls you just don't need to be running into. It is a matter of carefully evaluating who you are and who your clientele is. Most important, learn that while building and maintaining a client base is never easy, you should never, never give up."

HERE'S another bookstore idea. Buy a few magazines you've never read before. Maybe they're a motorcycle magazine, a family publication, and a magazine for seniors. As you flip through, let your creativity be sparked by these unfamiliar topics. How might this demographic benefit from your legal expertise?

MAINTAIN a global viewpoint. What trends may affect your practice? Being nimble enough to switch, say, from real estate deals to workouts and foreclosure prevention can sustain your practice throughout economic ups and downs. Keep an eye out for events and concerns that could affect your practice's viability or present new opportunities.

ASSESS your strengths and your position in the market. For example, if you decide you want to develop a practice in a specific area, you'll need to answer these questions:

● Do you have the skills necessary to do the work successfully?

● Are there other fields that might be more profitable or desirable?

● Do you have a base of practice on which to build?

● Do you have contacts that might help you build a practice base in that area?

● Does this practice area offer relatively easy entry, or is it saturated?

"I still track all new clients. You may think most of your business comes from a certain type of source, but with tracking, you may be surprised to learn that when you look at dollar amounts, it comes from another."

SOMETIMES you can segue into a lucrative practice by starting on the other side. For example, if you want to work in employment law, it may be easier to learn the area by doing plaintiff work with the help of an experienced co-counsel. With sufficient experience and expertise, you can market yourself on the management side.

SOME firms have prospered by specializing in very narrow areas. One woman lawyer with specialized knowledge of the burgeoning legal area of medical marijuana calls herself "L.A.'s Dopest Attorney." Consider whether you can identify and have the skills to service an unsatisfied demand.

Many lawyers, especially those new in practice, are reluctant to send any potential client away. That's a mistake. Take only the clients who fit

your profile. Send all the others to other lawyers and let them know what kind of clients you're looking for. The referrals you get back will more than compensate for those you sent.

Record the Plan

Know what your market is, determine where you want to fit into it, and then come up with a coherent plan for reaching your goals. That's the formula adopted by successful women rainmakers. As simple as it sounds, though, many lawyers find that their aspirations are rather nebulous until they put them in a document. Committing a marketing plan to writing, and differentiating short-, medium-, and long-term goals, gives you a benchmark for measuring your progress and determining whether your goals today are the same as they were a year ago or five years ago.

W E'VE all heard that chestnut, "If you fail to plan, you are planning to fail." Resolve today to set aside time to create your written marketing plan. Studies show that entrepreneurs who have a written business plan do better financially than those without such a plan. It can be as simple as handwritten notes on a legal pad. You can purchase marketing plan software and find sample plans on the Web.

D EFINE your target market and the tools you will use to reach that market. Set verifiable and specific goals—*e.g.*, "one new case a month from increased visibility in the north suburban market by writing a family law column in the neighborhood newspaper." Include specific actions that must be taken to achieve the goal and time lines for reaching the objectives. Review and revise your plan frequently. Analyze and change what doesn't work.

THE most important part of the marketing plan is a section outlining objectively verifiable goals. Examples are "two new product liability cases in the coming year" and "increase gross revenues 15 percent for the year." The more specific your goal, the better. "Improve client relations" is not an objectively verifiable goal. "Develop a client questionnaire and distribute by May 1" is.

EVEN in-house and government lawyers need to market. In-house personnel have three choices: forego legal advice, go to outside counsel, or use in-house lawyers. Market to in-house personnel so they know who you are and feel comfortable talking to you. Cultivate a reputation as a facilitator, not a "deal killer." Many employees are reluctant to contact internal counsel for a variety of reasons, but perhaps the most common is that they don't recognize that there is a legal problem. Frequent contact with your in-house clients will bring you information to alert you to legal problems sooner.

HERE is the plan of a lawyer seeking tort defense business. The target market niche has been defined as insurance carriers, risk-management companies, and major self-insureds. This rainmaker has collected information from industry journals and the state department of insurance to create a list of prospective clients. This is a file within the marketing plan folder and includes an activity log, where the attorney notes all her ideas and activities by date. Her goals are as follows:

Complete one marketing task every day.

Short-Term Goals (Six Months)
- Make one new contact per week.
- Follow up by telephone on contacts made in recent trip to St. Louis.
- Attend one bar association meeting per month.
- Send out at least one press release.

Medium-Term Goals (One Year)
- Have personal caseload of at least ten cases from at least one carrier.
- Visit current risk-management company client in Atlanta.
- Visit major airline prospect in New York City.

Long-Term Goals (Five Years)
- Partnership

DEFINE the goal and define the way to reach that goal: the means and the ends. The plan of a plaintiff's personal injury attorney who wants to start or increase her medical malpractice caseload might include the following:

Means
- Hire a Web designer to revamp our Web page to spotlight new practice emphasis within the next thirty days; complete redesign in ninety days.
- Research banner ads on *www.lawyers.com* for medical malpractice cases in my city within thirty days.

At first, setting aside time on a daily basis may seem impossible in your busy world, but with practice, marketing will become habitual.

◊ Create a short article for *www.Plaxo.com* and upload same within sixty days.

◊ Go to lunch once a week with another lawyer who may be a referral source.

◊ Join the medical malpractice subcommittee of the bar association within thirty days; attend at least 75 percent of the meetings over the next twelve months.

◊ Report all favorable medical malpractice case dispositions to the appropriate news media, including the local lawyers' paper, within forty-eight hours.

Ends

◊ Bring in five new medical malpractice cases within the next six months.

◊ Increase number of new medical malpractice cases to two per month for the six months after that.

After you reach the goal of two new malpractice cases a month, increase the target to three or four a month for the next twelve-month period.

THE degree of formality appropriate for your plan depends largely on how many people will rely on it. If you're the only one who will use the plan, a folder in your word processing program will do. Save short-, medium-, and long-term goals as separate files. Create a file for your budget and another to log your marketing activities.

A MARKETING budget should reflect a review of your financial records and a consequential commitment to spending a

certain percentage of last year's revenue on marketing. Decide what marketing tools the money will be spent on—*e.g.,* advertising, brochure design, printing. Follow through and follow up. Survey clients and others about their reactions to your efforts.

S MART business practices may include borrowing money to start or expand a law practice. Your banker or your firm's marketing committee will want to see your business plan, including projections on where the business will come from to repay the loan or budget allocation. If you are using your marketing plan as part of your presentation to a lender or other decision maker, naturally you will want to present it as attractively as possible.

Surveys show a high degree of dissatisfaction among lawyers, especially among women lawyers. Being a rainmaker is not a guarantee of job satisfaction, but the benefits and prestige that result from controlling your own business go a long way toward ensuring personal career fulfillment. Planning can get you there.

Choosing the Means to Reach the Ends

The choices can be overwhelming—a plethora of Internet advertising, print media, television, radio, and even outdoor advertising such as mobile and stationary billboards, bus signs, and ad benches. What will attract your target clientele? Keep your plan focused. Carefully consider a handful of marketing efforts and track the return. Adjust the plan as necessary. Every outreach may not result in a landslide of business, but don't get discouraged. Woody Allen said, "Eighty percent of success is showing up." Keep at it.

> **I started getting in to the office a half hour earlier to make time to check on my social media sites and read the additional e-mail I get from discussion groups.**

Not every marketing outreach will be successful; some may be dismal failures.

Keep a log of your marketing activities, and set a specific date to compare your progress to your goals.

Here are three ingredients for successful marketing:

- Internet visibility
- Repeated contacts with public and peers
- Competent and caring client service

Blawgs, which are blogs (Internet public journals) with legal content, can spark your creativity if you feel that you have run out of ideas. Solos can benefit from ***http://buildasolopractice.solopracticeuniversity.com/***, ***www.myshingle.com***, or ***www.lawbizblog.com***, among others.

One theory is to only use marketing tools with which you are comfortable. Teach if you enjoy it. Don't try it if you don't. The same holds true for writing articles, television ads, or any marketing tool you can think of. On the other hand, even if you are tech adverse, every lawyer needs to consider how to use the marketing power of the Internet. You don't need to become a computer engineer to be tech-savvy enough to communicate with current and potential clients.

Consider the search terms your niche market is likely to be using and how you can use these keywords in your different means of outreach. Lard your Website and press releases with those keywords. Use them in social media posts. Electronic tags, words and phrases likely to be used by would-be visitors to your site, can heighten the Web visibility of the subject matter, the firm, and its members. SEO—search engine optimization—is the name of the game.

In a small firm, partners can assign each other marketing tasks; *e.g.*, contact three former clients we have lost touch with.

WHAT is the best way to reach your target market? Analyze your own strengths. Are you an effective public speaker? Do you enjoy writing? If you agree to produce a weekly column, but your inclination, ability, and time commitments prevent you from reliably meeting deadlines, you may have done yourself more harm than good. A blog without regular posts is an unread blog. If time is your strength, Internet social media, seminars, and speeches might be the best exposure of your practice.

Working the Plan

A widespread theory says it takes six contacts to make a sale. Keep contacting that potential client. Keep publicizing your practice. When clients need a lawyer, they often contact the one they heard about most recently. Make sure it's you.

HOW often does a rainmaker market? The answer is every day. This isn't as onerous as you might think. The best marketing techniques are simple daily tasks, such as reading and forwarding articles of interest to clients. It's getting out of the office. It's planning.

MARKETING is an exceedingly slow process. You can make a successful presentation to two hundred people, everyone is clapping and the evaluations are terrific, and you're sure the phone will be ringing off the hook. But Monday morning, but nothing happens. On the other hand, you might have people calling you who say they took your course fifteen years ago and they kept the handout.

A lot of marketing is attitude. If you think you can't attract business, you won't.
The secret of success is following the lesson of The Little Engine That Could: *keep trying until you succeed!*

Visualize success.

FOLLOW-through is one of the most difficult marketing tasks. For example, let's say you were fortunate enough to obtain an invitation to deliver a major speech. Announce the event on your Web page and in your newsletter. Post an update on LinkedIn and tweet it on Twitter. Provide a link to the sponsor's Web page. If the sponsor hasn't posted information, follow up to help them gain valuable publicity. Your effort is only half effective if you spent a hundred hours preparing and writing extensive course materials but do not take the time to publicize it. After the seminar, rework the course materials into a short item for the local legal newspaper, where other lawyers who may become referral sources could read it. Allocate time and effort to achieve the biggest impact from every marketing outreach.

Survey clients and others about their reaction to your efforts.

Here is a sample log page for an attorney seeking corporate work who sets aside one morning a week for marketing:

Prospects

1.	ABC Products Corp. 123 Main St. Aliso Viejo, CA 92656 062/555-9876	Contact client Tom Brown. E-mail bounces back; no longer with company, now with Big & Huge in San Francisco. New CFO is Bob White—left voicemail and sent follow-up e-mail. (Follow-up date logged.)

2.	Honeybee Laboratories Industrial Park Metropolis, Georgia 34567 123/555-4321.	Referred by Betty Lou. Spoke with John Smith, who says he does all foreseeable legal work in-house. *To do:* • Thank-you message to Mike Morris for Herman referral • Make lunch date with Bob Carson.

" I HEARD one person say that you should spend 20 percent of your time marketing. Boy, that's a lofty goal. It's hard when you are in a crunch, but you have to do it. As women rainmakers who are trying to develop their own book of business and to get that independence, it is important. It is not going to happen overnight. The plan you put into effect today will take a long time to come to fruition. Some things may happen quickly; for others, it might be years before it results in a client. Start tomorrow."

Chapter 2

Image

You never get a second chance to make a first impression. How many times have you heard that one? Women, particularly, seem to be judged frequently on how they look rather than on what they do. Take a good look in the mirror and consider what impression you make. Do you exude confidence, knowledge, and power? What about your office, your business cards, and all the trappings which convey who you are?

Who Are You Anyway?

Your first step must be to analyze yourself. Who are you? What do you feel comfortable doing? It makes no sense to wear somebody else's "clothes" if they don't fit you. On the other hand, my experience tells me that sometimes you have capabilities that you're unaware of. I had no clients for five years while in a prior firm. Now I have a well-established practice. I didn't change. I was the same person, but my sense of self and what I needed to do changed. I think anyone can start from zero and create a practice if you're competent, imaginative, and enthusiastic and you put your energy into it.

GOOGLE yourself. What picture emerges about this person? If the results are sparse or out-of-date, start working on heightening your Internet profile. One way to do this is by

creating a free personal profile at *www.google.com/profiles*. You can also get your firm on Google maps without charge at *www.google.com/local/add*.

Because you are a rainmaker, people may be searching for information about you at any time. You're not going to do something that you don't want somebody to gossip about later—and that includes Internet postings. If there are unfortunate images swirling around the ether, you can try to remove them. However, even if the owner of the page is cooperative, it may be too late. Results come up in order of relevance to the query. Creating lots of good professional images can help push old, undesirable ones to the bottom of the results. Unfortunately, it may be hard to drown out a Website that's getting lots of hits—another reason to remember that once on the Web, the information—or image—can haunt you forever.

Studies show that men still dominate the highest paying positions in the business and legal worlds. That doesn't mean, of course, that you should try to become something you're not. Women rainmakers know themselves well. The key to success, they advise, is to be yourself. Don't worry about trying to determine what it is that the guys do that works for them. Don't worry about trying to adopt the dress or the mannerisms or the speech habits of the women in the office who made partner. Know your strengths, and make sure they're projected by your personal demeanor and your professional trappings.

Assess how you are perceived within your firm. Others must feel confident about bringing you in on a matter.

IMAGE

Evaluate positioning yourself, staying away from killer partners (the ones who seem out to "murder" your career), and affiliating with a mentor.

I SPENT years trying to be a conservative male, and obviously for a woman it was an impossible task. Having been in private practice now for nearly four years, I find that the friends that I developed inside client companies are the people that I really let get to know me, rather than the people for whom I put on a face, trying to resemble the people I saw being successful. And these friends became wonderful clients.

V IEW your gender as an advantage that helps you stand out from the crowd. Don't try to be a man clone.

Deciding whether to emphasize your gender is an important threshold issue. Some women lawyers specifically market themselves as female legal professionals. Typically these are family lawyers. However, many women—though not overtly—remind clients of the advantages of their gender. These might include putting the other side off guard or just being a good listener.

A S a solo, you can afford to do only certain work, and you don't want to attract the whole universe. Being a solo carries the implication that you're going to be doing the work—the client will be dealing with you and not with a huge entity. That is a selling point.

I N *My Fair Lady*, Henry Higgins sang, "Why can't a woman be more like a man?" Any discussion of the traits of lawyers

Develop the image that you are a good rainmaker, and you will be perceived as one.

typed by gender is necessarily flawed. There are aggressive women lawyers and men who are good listeners; women with scientific or military backgrounds and men who are soft-spoken. If appealing to the market's image of women lawyers—whatever that may be—works for you, great. Whether to play the gender card as part of your marketing scheme depends greatly on whether you feel you can deliver whatever you see as the implied promise of such a marketing program.

THE illusion of success is important. In response to "How's it going?" say "Business is fabulous," rather than "Things are slow." Fake it till you make it. Stop being so modest!

CLIENTS care that their lawyers *tried*, regardless of whether the case was won or lost. (Presumably you properly advised the client along the way.) Let the client see all the effort you expend on his or her behalf. Send the client copies of everything you receive or produce.

INSPIRE confidence by telling success stories. Explain how you helped clients in situations similar to the listener's. Look like a winner.

IMAGINE that you're at your own funeral! Your friends and family, your professional colleagues, and the people from your church or some civic organization in which you're a member are going to talk about you and what they remember of you. Imagine what you want to hear them say. Then work backward to where you want to go with your life from here. How do your professional circumstances and professional goals fit with your life goals? You must be comfortable with yourself, in touch with who you are and where you want to go, before marketing tips about developing client relations, maintaining client relations, and utilizing and building networks will work for you.

Lovely to Look At

"'I saw your picture. You are hot!' I never really know what to say to a telephone opening like that. Inevitably, I picture the male caller as nerdy and middle-aged. My professional photo, which appears on our Website as well as other sites, shows me in a business suit. Yes, I'm smiling, and of course I wanted to look as good as possible, but this wasn't what I was aiming for. Usually I simply say thank you or something self-deprecating like, 'I wish I still looked like that' or 'That picture was taken on a good day.'"

Managing your electronic and real-time image sometimes can be a challenge.

PICTURES do matter. When you deal with someone on the phone, isn't the communication enhanced if you can picture the person on the other end of the line? Spend the money to get a good professional photo taken.

An ad in the state bar journal showed a female supine on a desk with one leg dangling from it, facing the viewer, a stiletto-heel pump on the foot. The hem of the skirt of the business suit was midthigh. In later interviews, this professional woman (she provides some kind of litigation support services) said her business skyrocketed once she started running the ad. Apparently, sex still sells.

Have a sense of humor.

MAKE sure your clothes fit and are in good repair. A client told me, "You always look so well put together—I know you are going to handle my files with the same care and attention to detail." I was thrilled. On the other hand, I remember an interviewee whose blouse didn't close, exposing her bra. The woman had apparently gained weight and was wearing clothes a size too small. To my mind, she didn't look professional. If you have trouble pulling outfits together, you are not sure exactly what is and is not "business casual," or you just want to be fashion-forward while staying professional, call on the personal shopper at a major department store. The services are free. Let her know if you are on a budget. No personal shopping service in your town? Organize a girls' outing with your sisters, best friends, or anyone else who might be good in this capacity—the ones with taste and who aren't afraid to give you an honest opinion.

JUST as not every practice area responds to the same marketing technique, not every public image will be productive for every woman. For corporate accounts and sophisticated purchasers of legal services, looking like a "babe" may get attention from the men, but you need to back that up with an extra measure of competence and smarts.

DOES competing with men mean that you have to walk around in a gray flannel suit and a white shirt? No, it doesn't. Developing a distinctive look is fine. But consider the personal image statement you make as you are out and about on your daily activities—and not just from Monday to Friday. I was with my husband at the mall one weekend when we ran into a client who was with her mother, and I felt just fine about it. I didn't second-guess my wardrobe or appearance, because I knew that I was "dressing the part," to a point, every day.

To blend or not to blend. For some of us, that is the question. What is appropriate dress in one legal niche or locale may not be appropriate in another. Some lawyers will want to preserve an image by wearing business suits. Others will fit in best with their clients by sticking with business casual.

Some men can adopt far-out fashions with success: ponytails, cowboy regalia in northern climes, and feminine-looking fur coats. Regrettably, though, women are still best advised to adopt a conservative look. Since a good rainmaker attracts business everywhere she goes, plan on keeping the conservative persona for a long, long time.

PUBLICIZING your contact information has its own dilemmas, including economic and personal safety aspects. Using a post office box has always been a way to deter unwanted visits, but it's pretty easy to track someone's home address and phone. Depending on your practice area, you will want to be extra careful about how you manage (to the extent you can!) your contact information. Bots roam the Internet searching for e-mail addresses and fax numbers to send you junk. You can set up your Web page so that people can e-mail you without knowing your actual e-mail address. Consider declining to provide your fax number when subscribing to Websites.

> **A career woman has to look like a lady, act like a man, and work like a dog.**

Buy your name as a domain— e.g., www.Miriam Hildebrand.com— before someone else does.

Your Office

Take a look at your office. Is your reception room attractive? Are the periodicals appropriate? Art with legal themes, bar association informational brochures, and laudatory plaques and certificates all reassure the current and potential clients in your office.

BESIDES your firm's brochure, consider informational brochures for your waiting room if that fits your practice. Many bar associations and commercial vendors publish these for bulk purchase. Usually they deal with consumer and personal law issues such as buying a home, kids and the law, issues for seniors, or what to do if arrested. Some pamphlets also address small-business issues.

KEEP copies of articles and columns you've had published in a notebook in the reception area. Clients are usually impressed and sometimes will retain you for work in an area they hadn't realized you handle.

USE technology as a marketing tool. Let clients know that your computer systems are state of the art, that you spend the money to stay on the leading edge to better serve your clientele. Ask questions about enhancing compatibility with your clients' systems. Then make sure you do indeed utilize your equipment to its full potential.

Brand: You

What is your brand? You say you don't have one? Oh, but you do—it's your name.

"Branding" is the mantra of legal marketing. This conjures up notions of slogans and logos. While that may be part of branding, all branding really means is this: what is the image people think of when they hear your name or the name of your firm? Think about it. Aren't there certain lawyers or firms in your town whose name alone has taken on a secondary meaning? You can probably immediately name the premier plaintiff personal injury lawyer or intellectual property firm. Their names have become a brand for their specialty. What does your name stand for?

IF you choose to use a slogan and logo to make your name— *i.e.*, your "brand"—memorable, develop a plan for consistent usage. The colors, typeface, and perhaps size should be consistent on your Website, letterhead, business cards, and other firm materials. When visitors enter your office, the firm's name display should be consistent as well.

YOUR business card is the one item you probably give to everyone. What does it say about you? Consider paper grade and color and print style. Make sure the print is large enough to read easily.

YOUR stationery and business card convey an image of who you are. What about a dignified logo for use on your stationery, business cards, checks, and advertising? A scales of justice logo is pretty standard and can be ordered through just about any printer. A computer graphics consultant can inexpensively design a custom logo. Use the highest quality product you can afford.

USE the signature function for your e-mail message to make it easy for people to contact you through any medium—at the bottom of each message, provide your address, fax, phone, and Website URL. You also can include a short message with your signature. For a while I used "Free CLE at Ringler Radio— New program every 2 weeks" as a hyperlink to the Ringler Radio Website, promoting my company's Internet radio programming.

YOU can use a picture of your business card as your signature. Card Scan is a business card scanning machine, and the software lets you easily create a scan of your own card for use as your e-mail signature. Other such machines may also have this feature.

WHETHER you use electronic postage or a postage meter, you can include a marketing message with each letter. For the postage meter, you would purchase a custom-made "slug." If your firm has a slogan, use it here. Some businesses use a patriotic message, such as "United We Stand." Don't use your firm name, because that is already in the return address.

CHECK your state's ethical rulings on use of a trade name that describes what you do. A friend of mine has had great success promoting her practice as the Women's Law Center.

DO you have a personal trademark? One successful woman rainmaker with a bankruptcy practice wears a gold and diamond scales of justice brooch every day. Another well-known woman wears a hat every day. Trademarks make you memorable. They set you apart from the crowd and work as conversation pieces.

Chapter 3

Networking and Social Media

You've been networking all your life. Networking is simply building a circle of contacts. The more people you know, the more likely you are to get business from among those contacts. Don't overlook the networks you already have. Your friends, neighbors, and former classmates from every level represent important networking resources.

Rainmakers constantly network. Effective networking means making contacts in all areas of your life—professional, civic, social, academic—and keeping up with friends old and new, lawyers and non-lawyers. Whether it's a bar activity, a charity event or electronic discussion group, your participation gives you valuable exposure that may pay off when you least expect it.

The Power of the Web

Networking has gotten both easier and more complicated with the advent of Internet social media. Just because you have hundreds of

"friends" on Facebook doesn't mean you have someone to go with you to the mall or, more important from a professional standpoint, to refer you business. Some of the most respected professional marketers have admitted they are still trying to figure out how to transform time spent on social media into revenue.

FACEBOOK, LinkedIn, Twitter, YouTube, and whatever the next big social networking thing is, offer you the opportunity to raise your Internet profile without financial expenditure. Don't underestimate the time commitment, though. If you allow, say, an hour a day for marketing, be sure to include your time on these sites as well.

POTENTIAL clients, including corporate counsel, are checking out lawyers on social media sites. Some firms, in recognition of this new reality, have established policies for lawyers' pages. Does your firm have a policy? If not, consider spearheading the effort to create one.

LinkedIn seems to be the most business-oriented of the social media sites. There are a number of ways to elevate your LinkedIn presence:

◊ First, fully complete your profile. The more positive information you can provide about your services, your background, and you as an individual, the more likely the viewer will consider you a possible service provider. When clients ask, "How can I thank you enough?," suggest they provide a LinkedIn recommendation for your profile.

- Second, find and join LinkedIn groups that will allow you to demonstrate your expertise. You can display the logo of the groups you join on your profile page, but if there are too many, the important ones may get lost in the crowd, so display the logos that are most pertinent. One way to find appropriate groups is to search the pages of people you want to network with and see what groups they belong to. You can search for those people by industry, company, and geography through Advanced Search. You will automatically be notified when someone in your network joins a group. Consider joining that group yourself.

- Third, start and participate in discussions in those groups. Your goal should be to provide helpful information, not blatantly advertise. By demonstrating your proficiency in the subject, readers can then click through to your profile and from there to your firm's Website. If you see an interesting post in a discussion, check out that person's profile. If it looks like someone you want to follow you (and you want to follow), request permission to add him or her to your network.

- Last, be generous in recommending others.

The information on a social media Website is unlikely to be the last word in a potential client's investigation. It is just one more brick in building your marketing image.

D ON'T rush past your home page on LinkedIn. The right column will show you how often your profile is coming up in search results and how many people have viewed your profile. You may be able to figure out who they are with a basic

account, but perhaps not if the description is too generic. If you are not showing up in search results as often as you would like, try tweaking your profile to use more keywords and phrases that match likely searches.

How "friendly" do you want to be on Facebook or other social media sites? Do you accept everyone who wants to electronically befriend you? Many people do. While you can locate potential business prospects on social media sites—*e.g.*, geographically or through interest groups—and then send requests to connect, I would suggest that you be discreet in sending and accepting invitations. For example, I am not sure there is any benefit to connecting with other lawyers in your firm. Many times, your most worrisome competitors are the other lawyers in your own firm. Why would you want to share your marketing outreaches with them? Besides, in some organizations, there may be political reasons to avoid the jealousy that sometimes arises when a lawyer gets attention that someone else covets. It's bad enough that once your message is in the ether your outside competitors may be able to get their hands on it and piggyback on your creative efforts. Choose your connections wisely. There is nothing wrong with ignoring or declining an invitation. If you seek to connect with people you don't know and they indicate they don't know you, you may find yourself blocked from extending further invitations without meeting further requirements, such as providing the invitee's e-mail address.

F ACEBOOK has made strides in reaching out to the business user by offering pages, also known as Fan Pages, and groups. You can also publicize events, such as firm seminars, through Facebook. Manipulating Facebook for these purposes is not necessarily intuitive. One source for keeping current on

all Facebook has to offer is *The Zen of Social Media*, which promises continuous online updates.

Twitter seems to spark the most disagreement among lawyers about its usefulness. Many lawyers find it completely inappropriate for reaching their clientele. Others, however, both BtoC and BtoB, claim great success with Twitter as part of a comprehensive, fully-planned marketing outreach package. They counsel using Twitter to drive traffic to the firm Website and to use it in conjunction with other media. Link to other Websites to magnify the range of shared information, but be sure the articles are relevant and viewable—not a PDF download.

Twitter is different. Unlike the other mainstream social media and communications tools, Twitter allows quicker exchanges among more people. In this way, you might be fooled to communicating as you would in a face-to-face conversation, but don't forget this is the Internet. Assume your communications will be public forever.

To tweet or not to tweet. Even U.S. senators are using Twitter, so somebody must be paying attention. If Twitter is foreign to you, consider picking up a book like *Social Media for Lawyers*, published by the American Bar Association Law Practice Management Section, or *Twitter Marketing for Dummies* by Kyle Lacy. Developing a Twitter following requires building a Twitter profile and creating opportunities for people to start following you through your other marketing outreaches, such as a link on your Web page and in your e-mail signature. One way to learn this medium is to start following industry and legal leaders and see what they do. For your goals—at least on your business account—tweeting about

where you ate lunch or where you are going on your next vacation is irrelevant. What you can do is announce seminars, host events, hold chats, and reference articles and press releases. Twitter has its own language: *hashtags, retweets, fans, #FollowFriday*. Look up terms as you find them.

W HAT are your competitors doing? Do some sample Internet searches and see what you get. Will something similar work for you?

Actively seek out discussion sites on legal and trade Websites.

L EGAL discussion site Solosez (***www.abanet.org/soloseznet***), is so popular that the Website offers suggestions for managing the e-mail flood from its 3,500 members (and not just solos). They are a resource, a sounding board, and a valuable referral source.

M OST law schools and colleges maintain online alumni directories, an invaluable networking tool.

T HE newest social media tool creating buzz is—wait for it— Buzz. You can find it at ***www.google.com/buzz***. Log into Gmail (create a free account if you don't have one) and navigate to Buzz.

What is the most appropriate way to mine your potential client base? Will corporate executives follow your tweets? Will financially stressed homeowners facing foreclosure see a LinkedIn discussion? Old media may still be the best way to reach potential clients who are unlikely to

search for a lawyer through social media sites. These individuals may be older or do not have ready access to a computer or just consider the Internet an inappropriate way to connect with a legal professional.

Look 'Em in the Eye

It's easy to network through your computer or Smartphone, but chances are you are not building the productive relationships that result from face-to-face contact. Get out of your chair, and get involved with real people.

Face-to-face contact remains important. Young lawyers proficient in social media still need to get out of the office to market. They can get involved in any organization they find interesting or rewarding: politics, church, the health club.

Organizations Galore

Besides knowing how to network, you have to figure out where to do it. Answer: be a joiner.

Which Organization?

Many organizations will welcome your participation. Your goal is to choose the one that will be most fulfilling both personally and professionally in light of your limited time. Here are some options:

- *Bar associations*: your best referrals come from other lawyers
- *Women's business groups*: mixed or single industry (*e.g.*, Women in Real Estate)
- *Philanthropic*: charity boards
- *Religious or ethnic*: don't forget your church, synagogue, or other religious gathering place
- *Traditional "old boy" networks*: *e.g.*, Kiwanis, Rotary Club

Just joining isn't enough. Active participation through regular attendance at meetings and committee leadership distinguishes you as a go-getter. Of course, if you take on a task, you must complete it competently. The idea is to give people a chance to get to know you for the bright, capable person you are.

Be Choosy

Join selectively. Choose an organization in which you have a genuine interest. Others will bore you. Besides, it's hard to work up enthusiasm for a goal you don't really care about.

More is not necessarily better. If you spread yourself too thin, you can't make a meaningful contribution anywhere. You'll just be a name on a mailing list, and that doesn't benefit you as a rainmaker at all.

Appropriate Expectations

Give any organization a fair chance. After all, there was something about it that originally attracted you. But if you discover that the membership isn't right for you demographically, or you're just not enjoying it, quit and move on. There are so many organizations, you're sure to find another that better meets your needs.

Don't be pushy with other members. The soft sell always works best. Let people know what you do, but appreciate people for their diversity, their friendship. If you value people only as prospective clients, your mercenary attitude will quickly be obvious and turn them off. On the other hand, let people know (within ethical bounds) that you do want them as clients and their referrals. Some people think if you project a successful image that you don't need any more clients!

Don't expect results right away. A year after starting active participation is not too long to wait. In the meantime, enjoy the organization's activities. You may be surprised at the personal satisfaction you derive.

JOIN the chamber of commerce. Get out and meet your fellow businesspeople. Shake hands, pass out cards. Offer to speak, work on a committee. Get your name known in the community.

STAY in touch with your alumni association—both undergrad and law school. Many schools sponsor alumni social events. If you are in the geographic area, your law school may offer a full calendar of events ranging from cocktail parties to celebrity speaker events to continuing legal education courses. Your fellow alums are a potential referral gold mine.

THINK of the people that you come in contact with at your place of worship and during leisure activities as possible clients or as possible referrals. Even if people you meet there have professional activities that are completely irrelevant to yours, let them know what you do. If they are your friends, they will likely refer another friend or family member in need of your particular skills.

THE U.S. Small Business Administration, in cooperation with state governments, sponsors Small Business Development Centers and Women's Business Centers. (See, *www.sba.gov/aboutsba/sbaprograms/onlinewbc*.) Get to know the staff at your local center, and learn about the programs they sponsor. Their clients can become yours.

MANY women attorneys report success from joining LeTip (*www.letip.com*). A LeTip chapter admits one of each type of professional and is dedicated to exchanging business leads.

CONSIDER joining a barter association. Barter associations provide a way to turn your excess time into income. Instead of cash, you will receive barter credits. Barter accounts are kept in dollars, and you will bill clients exactly as you would as if they were paying in cash. Of course, you must require any cost advance to be paid in cash, since your vendors are unlikely to be in the same barter exchange.

The benefit is that you have a built-in market for your services that would not likely have come to you otherwise. These members are part of your personal network and are likely to refer cash clients.

The downside is you are limited in your purchases to what you can buy from the other members. Also, the Internal Revenue Service taxes barter income the same as cash—when you receive it, not when you spend.

One rainmaker who belongs to a barter exchange reports the following: "I have purchased two phone systems for my office as I have grown through the years. I dictate over the phone to my backup barter secretarial service. I purchase everything from office supplies and business Christmas gifts to jewelry and art. I rented an apartment on barter and moved both my business and my household furnishings. I eat at barter restaurants and stay at barter hotels. There are dentists, accountants, chiropractors, and morticians in the exchange."

If you have a small-business practice and time on your hands, joining a barter exchange may open a new market to you.

NETWORKING is probably your most important source of marketing leads. Women's organizations can provide new

community contacts, opportunities for public speaking, and a forum to exchange ideas with other businesswomen. How many of these organizations are in your city?

- YWCA is the largest women's organization in the United States. Check your local facility for programs for businesswomen and entrepreneurs.
- Groups catering to women in business, management, construction, telecommunications, film, and in just about every other possible industry you would be interested in courting; these organizations provide a fertile networking ground not dominated by other lawyers.

EVEN churches and synagogues sponsor businesswomen's groups. Many women partners and solos consider the National Association of Women Business Owners the best of the bunch, because every member is a decision maker.

DOZENS of women's organizations, including the National Association of Women Lawyers (*www.nawl.org*), sponsor mentor and support programs. There is a specialized organization for almost every industry, such as Women in Film, Association for Women in Communications, Women in Technology International, Women's Shipping & Trade Association International. If you want to work with professionals in a specific industry, this may be a good way to start making contacts. Many universities, as well as the American Association of University Women, have these programs as well. This is a wonderful way to develop relationships. Be creative in your investigation, as programs can come and go.

WHAT if you've looked around your community and found that there is no high-level businesswomen's organization? Start one! Have lunch with those you believe will form the nucleus of your group. Decide how to proceed, and divide up the tasks.

If you have a good-sized conference room, you can call the organizational meeting in your office. Alternatively, consider getting space in a community building or the banquet room of a restaurant. The problem with the last suggestion is that the restaurant will probably require a deposit, impose a minimum fee, and require attendees to purchase a meal. If you don't get the expected turnout, there could be a financial loss.

Publicize your budding group through the local paper, community access cable television, bulletin board notices, and every other way you can think of. Consider membership requirements: years in business, work in a specific industry, and business ownership are possibilities. Maybe you will welcome any working woman.

Expect to put in some serious time to get the group going. The payoff will be in shared knowledge, networking, and clients.

GET active in community affairs as a way to promote yourself and your skills. Every charitable organization needs volunteers and, more important, can use your skills and talents on governing boards. Practicing law puts things in perspective and trains you to make well-informed decisions quickly. Charitable and community boards and committees need people with these abilities. Usually other board members are movers and

shakers in the community whom you may never otherwise meet. What you do for these groups can be the basis for press releases. The best part is that it doesn't feel like marketing.

Bar Associations and Lawyer Groups

Get active in one or more bar associations. The best way is through the special interest groups. People within the smaller groups tend to be compatible and friendly. Getting your name on the membership roster of a substantive law section or committee signals your expertise and genuine interest. Additional benefits of membership are writing opportunities, committee activities, conferences, and seminars—all excellent ways of generating business.

Y our bar association can promote you. Bar associations love workers. You have to get active. Your bar association can give you legitimacy and can give you visibility. I'm very nice to the association staff. The staff like me, so the editor of the bar newspaper did a feature on me. The purpose of the article was to promote the association activities in which I was involved, but it also heightened my personal visibility in the legal community in a very favorable way. Don't take those staff people for granted; do not treat them with anything but respect and courtesy and affection, because they can help you a lot.

" I can't overemphasize the importance of getting involved in bar activities. One of the things I have done is take other lawyers who are in litigation sections in larger firms to lunch and dinner or whatever and tell them, 'I want your business.' Tell these lawyers that when they have conflicts in this

area, that's what you want. You are not trying to compete with them or take their clients away from them. Let them know you are there, and of course your reputation must precede you. They need to know you are available to take those conflict situations."

PRO bono work can be a marketing tool. If there is a prestige lawyer's organization in your town that does pro bono work, that may be the best networking opportunity. The price of admission is the pro bono case.

YOU also can enter a new practice area through your pro bono work. Nonprofit community organizations are likely to need all kinds of legal services but lack funds for paid counsel. You might offer to represent a citizens' group for a cause you believe in. Your bar association may have a committee that provides legal advice to starving artists.

"IF you don't have a niche within your local bar association, create one. We didn't have a bankruptcy law committee; I was involved in forming one, and you can guess who is chairperson of it."

JOINING U.S. Law Network (*www.uslaw.org*) was the best thing our firm ever did. As part of a consortium of firms, we can compete with the big guys, and our cross-referrals give us a national presence. Other national law networks include the International Society of Primerus Law Firms (*www.primerus.com*) and Meritas (*www.meritas.org*). Law Marketing Portal

(*www.lawmarketing.com*) maintains a list of such networks. Thoroughly investigate before committing—and that includes the financial commitment—as not all organizations billed as networks are created equal. Commercial Law League of America (*www.clla.org*), for example, is more like a specialized bar association than a consortium of firms helping each other.

MANY professional organizations now sponsor women's retreats. Defense Research Institute and U.S. Law Network are two. These getaways allow women to find and help each other within organizations where women remain a minority.

BECOME a mediator or arbitrator. This gives you access to a whole new group of lawyers. Involvement in alternate dispute resolution is a great way to get to know judges, other lawyers, and potential clients. Many court systems will welcome you to their alternative dispute programs and may provide training.

See Every Person as an Opportunity

Strike up a conversation with the business traveler next to you on your next plane trip. Corporate financial guidelines require nearly everyone to ride in coach these days. You can network with bank presidents, environmental consultants, and corporate bigwigs of every stripe at fifty thousand feet.

" I ALWAYS pay to fly first class—out of firm funds, not the client's. This allows me to meet key people in a natural setting where they have plenty of time to get to know me."

"YOU just never know. I recently stopped for a fast-food lunch at a crowded food court with an outdoor patio. Since there were no empty tables, I asked a solo female diner if I could join her. It turned out that she was a manager at a company I had targeted for months. Though her department probably could not give me business, she had a personal relationship with those managers who had been ducking my calls for months, and she was able to facilitate an introduction."

IF you have a contact in one area of a very large corporation, you can ask your contact for names of employees who work in your target market area. Once you have a name, you have an inroad, and you can say, "So-and-so referred me to you."

IT'S a mistake to avoid socializing with low-level employees in a client organization, particularly if you are a junior person yourself. Take your peer to lunch, dinner, the symphony, the theater, the zoo, the botanic garden, or wherever. Just as you are progressing through your career, these people are progressing through theirs. Eventually they will be senior-level engineers or geologists or general counsels and valuable contacts.

"MEN are raised to integrate the social and business parts of their lives. For women, there's a learning curve. You need to learn to socialize while you are at a trade association, or do business development while you are at a birthday party."

DON'T burn your bridges. Stay on good terms with former employers and opposing counsel. They can be significant referral sources.

**Personal contacts!
Meet as many people
as you can.**

Get to know your kids' teachers and the parents of their friends.

Your firm's vendors may be a source of business, either directly or by referral. Manage your vendor relationships as if every vendor were a potential client. Strike up a conversation about whether the vendor may be working with your target prospects. Consider multiplying the number of vendors you do business with to increase the likelihood of receiving reciprocal business.

Law students, start making your contacts and building your personal relationships with business and professional people while you are still in school. Join one to three targeted groups as a student member and become active in the group.

" This is a tip for those of you who came to the law as a second career. I kept up my contacts by writing a letter to former clients stating that I am now a lawyer, telling them I now do real estate property work, and asking that if they have a building they are buying or selling to please keep me in mind. I have gotten a lot of work that way. If you have had a prior association, even though you are not going to practice in that area, you still have those contacts."

Lawyer-to-Lawyer
Network with attorneys who are both very much senior and very much junior to you. Those junior people, especially the ones who are so successful that they go on to become governors or senators, will remember your kindnesses to them. So be kind to the goofball, low-end new per-

Send congratulations notes to other lawyers on their accomplishments.

son or marginal lawyer, because the benefit to you can be enormous. At the high end, all you do is ask, "How do you do this?" The senior attorneys will be flattered enough that they will spend an hour giving you notes and sending you business.

"MANY of us think that the place to get business is from other lawyers who are more experienced and have been around longer. But it's important for lots of reasons, including marketing, to befriend, do favors for, help out, and mentor younger lawyers. I have done that on many occasions, and I have found many of these younger lawyers have gone on to practice settings where they have business to refer out. They have remembered me and have been grateful for my help and have been a great source of business for me."

ONE law school alumni association has a mentoring program that pairs experienced and new attorneys. Experienced lawyers teach rainmaking and other practice management skills. Check if similar programs are available through your alma mater.

"OUR best sources were other lawyers who didn't do bankruptcy work. They would very often send lots and lots of work to us, and the guarantee was we would always send the clients back. We never took their clients."

Working the Room

This tip is called "meet and greet." Choose an organization you think you would like to be involved with. It might be an industry organiza-

tion; it might be a women's group. Happily, you can combine the two—
e.g., women in management, women in sales, women in architecture,
women in construction, women's bar associations. Find out the date for
the next open meeting and enter it into your calendar as high priority.

When you go to networking events, wear something with pockets.
Put the cards you are going to give in one pocket and the cards you get
in the other. If you go up to somebody and you have to fumble through
your purse, by that time the person has walked away. Have your business cards in your pocket and ready. When you get back to your office,
write down on the card the date and place where you met the person and
follow up with a letter or e-mail. Do it within a few days while the person still remembers who you are. Provide information on how you can
help. If you promised to send something, do it.

Most organizations provide name tags. One theory holds that you
should always put the tag on the right shoulder because when you move
to shake hands, it is the part that will go forward. The point is to make
the tag clearly visible to the onlooker. If it has a name you don't use
("Margaret" rather than "Peggy"), get out a pen and change it. Add your
company name if it is missing. At a national conference, write in your city.

The hardest part of "meet and greet" is going up to strangers in
groups. You feel like an outsider. It is hard, and it takes a lot of nerve to
go up to people and introduce yourself. Sometimes you find yourself
with some other outsider. One technique is when you find yourself with
some other outsider, act like you are an insider: take the other person by
the elbow and bring her over to the most important person in the room.
Say something like, "Paul President, I would like to introduce you to
Ann Oakley." Ann thinks you are great, and Paul is trying to remember
where he met you before, but it gets you in the group. That is also a way
for you to move from cluster to cluster in a group.

IF you are at all shy about the cocktail reception introduction thing, consider buying *How to Work a Room*, by Susan Roane. This book has some very concrete, practical, interesting tips that will help you overcome some of the inherent shyness that more junior lawyers feel about these types of situations.

How you shake hands is often the first impression you leave. How is your handshake?

Do's

- Some men are still reticent to a shake a woman's hand. Extend yours first if necessary.
- Keep your palm perpendicular to the floor.
- Keep four fingers together, thumb up.
- Take the other person's whole hand firmly into your whole hand.
- Shake one to three times—more gets silly.

Don'ts

- Don't curve your fingers down as if you expected your hand to be kissed.
- Don't loosen your hand as if it were a limp rag.
- Don't grip so hard it seems you're in an arm-wrestling contest.
- Don't use a two-handed handshake except to show affection—rarely in business.

PRACTICE a script for introducing yourself in a networking setting—a "cocktail party description," if you will. Some people call this an "elevator description" because it has to be short enough to be said in an elevator ride—as short as a few

words but no longer than two sentences. The description should be concrete and stated in terms of what a potential client needs or how a potential client can benefit from your service. Strive for action words, and be positive. For example, "I help injured people receive fair compensation" is more meaningful than "I'm a personal injury lawyer." Here are some others:

- "I'm a lawyer with Forthright & Honest. We protect your rights in court."
- "I help corporations comply with Delaware's unique corporate laws."
- "I provide cost-effective representation to small businesses like yours."

WHEN you give people your business card, put a note on it to remind the recipient of your conversation. Maybe include the date and where you were, *e.g.*, "CBA [City Bar Association] 7/6/2010" They are less likely to throw it away. When they see the card again and see the note, they will think of your conversation.

If you're bad at remembering names, write down some unique feature about that person on her card so you can later identify her.

BE able to discuss the news—especially sports—at networking events. While you want to stay away from those two infamous danger zones of politics and religion, being able to discuss current events gives you something to talk about and a common footing with those with whom you want to bond.

"We invite our referral sources for a breakfast; people are fresh that way."

Calendar dates to call others to go out for lunch just as you would calendar a reminder date on a case.

Send business to women professionals, and you are likely to get business and referrals in return.

THE mixologist at your party may be renowned, but take it easy on the alcohol. Nurse one drink or stick with nonalcoholic beverages. Intoxication may lead you to say or do something that will prevent your getting business from that group—and isn't that why you're there in the first place? Women who get drunk seem to get criticized more than men—and they can do things that are even stupider.

Eat!

Go out to lunch. You can't network with a sandwich at your desk. Call up a client, an old classmate, the new lawyer one floor down, or the new acquaintance you met at a seminar.

" EVERY month I go to a lunch with a number of, as it happens, women professionals and attorneys. To keep that from becoming just a friendly monthly lunch, you really have to follow up with the individuals in the meeting. I make it a practice to try, after the lunch, to pick out one of those people I have met to go one-on-one with. I contact her afterward and say, 'It was nice to have lunch with you. Let's get together, just you and me.' This way you can build a personal relationship with that person."

" TAKE advantage of every opportunity daily life presents. I recently had the opportunity to have lunch with executives of a potential client—an insurance company—where the head person was a woman. The other people at the lunch were men. One of the other people in my firm was very dominating in our conversation at lunch, and I didn't have an opportunity

to say very much. Afterward, I happened to be in the ladies' room with this woman and made my points there. Take every opportunity you can. It's the 'new girl connection.'"

Matchmaking

Refer business to your clients whenever you can. Let them know you were the source.

PUTTING clients together, matchmaking, is a great networking tool, but do not—*do not!*—brag about being or call another woman a yenta! Yenta means "a gossip" in Yiddish, not a matchmaker. (And it's a noun, not a verb.) To call a woman a yenta is an insult. I have heard women lawyers misuse this term on several occasions. This all got started because in the musical *Fiddler on the Roof*, the town matchmaker was named Yenta. It was a joke. If you don't know your Yiddish, don't use it.

I LIKE to refer clients to several possible lawyers. Then the clients can choose the location, gender, age, and price range that suit them best. After I make the referral, I call the lawyers whose names I provided to let them know that Mary Smith may be calling them on my referral. Whether Mary follows through or not, I've scored points with all those lawyers by having provided their names.

REALLY get to know your clients' business or occupation, even if you are representing them in an unrelated matter. Refer business to your clients whenever possible. They then benefit from knowing you separately from your legal work.

Synch your phone and your computer to keep your contacts' information with you on the road.

Even try to refer business to people who are not currently your clients. These people then know you are concerned about their business and will consider you in a positive light when their need for a lawyer arises.

M AKE friends with your doctor, dentist, chiropractor, or other health professional and refer patients to him or her. Then duplicate this technique with your accountant, financial planner, and stockbroker. Note that an agreement to swap clientele is an unethical fee-sharing agreement.

Follow Up

There are many ways to keep track of information about clients and prospects alike. Keep a simple list in Word or Excel, or use the contact manager in Outlook. Add your new contacts to your newsletter distribution list. Of course, you can buy more specialized contact-management applications. Don't delay entering information into your system while you get around to deciding what salutation to use, whether to send a holiday card, or if you should add the name to your newsletter circulation list. Do it promptly.

I ASSIDUOUSLY collect business cards from other lawyers, mediators, and business contacts and scan them into my card scanner. The results are amazingly accurate, but you can manually correct any errors. The data can be sorted by name, company, or date scanned. You can also create categories. When you are trying to remember someone, the business card scanner's program's versatility can help.

FOLLOW up your networking with a message repeating your pleasure in meeting your new acquaintance. If appropriate, indicate that you would be pleased to help that person with the legal issue you discussed briefly. Several business supply houses now sell informal cards printed with "Enjoyed meeting you" or "To follow up." You can also find similar greetings at the office supply store. It's so rare to get a personal letter that you will surely make an impression. Meticulously avoid outright solicitation of any individual's legal business.

Chapter 4

Communications: E-mail, Telephone, Snail Mail, and More

The more things change, the more they stay the same. Though the choices have multiplied, basic communication skills remain the cornerstone for successful client relationships.

How does your client want to be reached? Make sure you cover this point at intake. Phone, e-mail, U.S. post? Is that phone number a landline or a cell? What about text messages? What is appropriate for a thirty-year-old divorce client may be worthless to a seventy-year-old with questions about estate planning. Cell calls and texting may create charges that the client only wants if there is an emergency. Each method has its pluses and minuses. Some are quick; some are cheap. Some allow lengthy explanations but may miscommunicate due to the inability to convey tone.

As the ways to communicate increase, so do the challenges to do so effectively. When clients started using fax instead of U.S. post, the expected time for turnaround contracted. E-mail made it contract more. It's not only important to develop ways in your practice to communicate using the client's preferred medium, but also to foster reasonable client expectations.

E-mail

How savvy are you about "netiquette"? Many clients have bulging e-mail boxes and only want to hear from you on an as-needed basis. Not every electronic communication needs to be acknowledged with an e-mail response. Keep e-mail messages terse—preferably all on one screen. Don't send jokes unless you know they are welcome. Ask your clients about their e-mail preferences.

The author of an article in a law practice magazine wrote, "It is hard to imagine law practice without e-mail." Well, some of us do remember practicing law without e-mail quite well, not to mention without computers, fax machines, or word processors. While e-mail may be fast, it has its pitfalls. E-mail allows more detail than a voicemail message, but the writer's words may be perceived incorrectly or provoke disagreement. Tone is lost in e-mails. Something intended to be innocuous can be perceived as brusque or even insulting. Without the give-and-take of a phone conversation, an e-mail exchange can actually be slower in cementing an understanding or plan of action. Sometimes e-mail goes astray. A server doesn't let it go through due to size or content, or it ends up in the receiver's junk folder. Some receivers get hundreds of e-mail messages a day, and yours may get lost in the morass. In many companies, when someone leaves, it's as if those e-mails never existed. The person who has taken over the matter at your client may have no idea about what happened before her involvement because the e-mails are not accessible. It is often wise to use multiple media to make sure your advice and activities are on record.

ATTACHMENTS must be easy to open—PDF is the gold standard. Get software that allows you to convert to PDF. You also can convert any file to PDF format by "printing" it to a PDF converter. Sending attachments in TIFF (tagged image file format), BMP (bitmap), or other picture formats may result in them never being opened and a degree of frustration.

MULTIPLE e-mail addresses can help manage inbound communications. Office@lawfirm.com or mail@lawfirm.com can be used on your Website and business card. Someone should check this mailbox at least daily. You can initiate or provide your e-mail address for priority e-mail exchanges to and from Yourname@lawfirm.com, but don't subscribe to online services with Yourname@lawfirm.com.

Telephone

The most common client complaint is lack of responsiveness. Pick up your voicemail as frequently as you pick up messages from your secretary or receptionist. Return calls at least twice a day. Your secretary should always know where you can be reached.

IF you can't return a phone call, have your secretary call and say you're unavailable right now, but ask if anyone else can help. Or ask the client to explain fully what is needed, and your secretary will convey the information when you call in.

Many new clients will simply go on to the next lawyer on their list if they can't reach you.

If you're unavailable, you may want to have your secretary give the caller an appointment.

NOTHING is more effective than returning those phone calls the same day. If you are there until 6:30 or 7:00 p.m., clients will say, "I can't believe you are still at the office calling me." You may be calling them from home, but it doesn't make any difference. You still care enough to get back to them, and that's been one of the most impressive things I have been able to do, particularly with new clients.

MANY people hear your voicemail announcement every day. It's a great marketing opportunity, almost invariably wasted. I can figure out that you're on another line or not at your desk (or too busy to take my call), so don't waste my time. Slightly better is the familiar, "We're helping other clients." But how about being more specific? "I'm out of the office helping homeowners stay in their homes."

VOICEMAIL can be a big turnoff. Change your message frequently. Make sure the message gives instructions to allow talking to a human being, and ensure that that person will take a message, not send the caller back to voicemail.

CALLERS appreciate it when voicemail offers options, such as calling on the mobile phone or asking for someone else by name.

GIVE clients your home number. This is a "security blanket" for many clients. For better or worse, when there's an emergency, you'll be the one to get the call. Order conferencing and call-forwarding features for your home phone. Keep voicemail on whenever you are unavailable to take calls.

CONSIDER installing a toll-free phone number. Maintenance of the number is cheap, and it's more effective as well as cheaper to have someone call you back once than to have to make five or six calls to connect.

Have a direct dial line.

Answer your own phone whenever possible.

BE available. If clients are morning people, be there for them in the morning. If their biorhythms are high in the late afternoon, try to be available then. Use the forward option on your phone to get calls on your mobile unit. Another choice is to obtain technology that will allow your staff to patch calls through to you wherever you are.

"THERE are only a few things that distinguish one lawyer from another. One is service and another one is responsiveness. You can be a great lawyer, but if you don't return your telephone calls you are not going to keep the client. I have always made a point of being very responsive to clients and acting very interested in their own work; not just the case you are working on, but the totality of their business, so they feel you are there for them and you care about them. When they have other work, you get that work, and when they know of someone else who needs a lawyer, they will say, 'Boy, do I have a lawyer for you.'"

IF you don't like your voice, change it. A voice coach can help you get rid of that conspicuous accent or learn to speak at a different decibel. A voice coach taught me a new way to breathe to make my voice less harsh.

Smile when you talk on the phone.

It really does make a difference to your tone of voice and the reaction of others.

Billing

Think about the last bill you got in the mail. Chances are there were inserts advertising other products. If you get your bills electronically, there are links enticing you to learn about more than just your bill. Your invoice for legal services is a communication your client is likely to see on a regular basis. It should be professional and reflect value. Like your own creditors, you can also use your billing to include an insert or link with educational material or announcing a new firm member, service, or seminar.

OUR firm had an in-house program to teach marketing, which we thought was very effective. The modules covered things like listening skills, initial client interviews, and client complaints. Most of them, actually, were oriented toward eliciting information from clients. There was a module on cross-selling. Again, that employed listening communication skills to learn about marketing opportunities with existing clients. There was a module on billing as a marketing tool, with a variety of approaches to billing practices and retainers. Too often, attorneys just get the bill out on some form that was set up years ago. In my bills, I try to include a full description of the work being charged. If you simply say, "Will and trust: $X," that doesn't tell you very much. But if you say, "Analysis of family and financial facts, in-depth consultation with client," it shows the client what was involved. Another lawyer I know includes a cover letter that says something regarding the matter and personalizes the bill. I think this is a good marketing tip, too.

THE bills that come in with a short narrative that reminds the client what the lawyer did for the last month or three months or six months make a lot more sense to me and generate a lot more goodwill than the ones that come in without any kind of description.

BILLING can be an effective marketing tool, because the marketplace is now seeking billing arrangements that offer both clear trails of what it is outside lawyers have been doing and also arrangements besides hourly billing—*e.g.*, unit billing—as alternatives to try to control those costs.

To remind people that I want their business, I try to make it a practice that with every bill I send out, I not only write a little narrative, but I put a line at the end about how I'm here if there is anything else we can help the client with. I have had a couple people call me after they have gotten the bills and said something else has come up. The timing was such that it may or may not have had anything to do with our reminder, but in general, it can't hurt.

MANY billing software programs allow a comment to be placed on each bill that can be changed each month. A marketing message for an elder law firm might read, "Call for our new brochure on Social Security benefits." Bills rendered in December might say "Best wishes for the holiday season." The comment can call attention to the firm's new name or address or even a postage increase.

Here's the input of an in-house lawyer:

"One of the things that causes lawyers to lose business and is a real gripe among in-house counsel is when lawyers send us bills that include an increase in the hourly rate without having called to discuss it first. I can assure you the next time I send a matter out, I will not send it to the lawyer who has raised rates without notice. There need not have been a lot of money at issue. The rate may not be any higher than that of another firm we use. But just raising the rates by ten dollars at the end of the year and sending a little notice with the bill that the rate is now ten dollars more is not a way to do business with me.

"The way to do business with me is to discuss your need for a rate increase. We need to sit down and try to work out whether we are willing to pay more. I am budgeted, and part of my incentive pay is based on my managing my legal fees. I can't afford to get into circumstances where you have now raised the litigation costs. When I set up a budget with you, I expect you to stay within that budget and not to write me a letter to say we are going over budget and this is what is happening. Unfortunately, this happens all too frequently."

You may find helpful the American Bar Association book *How To Draft Bills Clients Rush to Pay.*

Greeting Cards and Notes

Keep a collection of greeting cards in the office. You can dash one off upon learning of a client's illness, marriage, job promotion, or a death in the family. Many companies now make cards specifically for use among business colleagues.

" A VERY simple thing I have done is sent Christmas cards to all past clients. I have had one client come in that I had previously represented on a small employment matter and hadn't seen him for a year or more. When he decided he wanted to get a divorce, he came in carrying the card saying, 'I'm glad I found this. My wife just left me, and now I need a divorce.'"

DON'T send greeting cards only at holidays. There is a line of cards called Corporate Courtesies (800/779-2779) that is a woman-owned company. They are very dignified navy, cream, or burgundy cards, and women rainmakers report very nice feedback. A commonly used card says, "Thank you for your referral." There is another one that says, "Enjoyed meeting with you."

IT'S amazing how much people do appreciate beautiful, thoughtfully chosen holiday cards. Even if the firm has a master list, keep a personal list for sending in your own name.

WORSE than not sending any cards at all is to send cards that simply have your name imprinted on them. One lawyer reports that she was taught this lesson rather severely the first year that she sent out imprinted cards without a personal signature. A furious client called to say, "If you don't have the time, and I'm not important enough to personalize the cards, don't waste everybody's time and money by doing this!" Obviously the lawyer was not pleased with this reaction, but it made her stop and think. She decided the client was right and now takes the time to sign all her cards.

NOT only should you personally sign every one of your holiday greeting cards, but always try to write some kind of personal note. Of course it is important to know your client's

Prepare for bulk mailings of newsletters and holiday cards by keeping your contact mail merge list up-to-date.

Remember what your mother taught you: write thank-you letters for everything.

(Or make thank-you calls immediately following the meeting or other occasion.)

business, but it is also important for clients to feel you are interested in them as people and know them individually and know what they are interested in so that you can personalize your relationship.

TECH-SAVVY clients may appreciate electronic greeting cards. Choose the ones with a small fee to avoid sending an advertisement with your card. Be sure you know your recipient. Some people find an e-card nothing more than an irritant and would better appreciate a traditional card sent through the mail.

"AS an in-house lawyer, I send congratulations cards to employees on their promotions or anniversaries. I send personal holiday cards in December."

"WHENEVER I get a referral from someone, I always write a thank-you for the referral, but I also note the referral in my file. When the matter is completed, I write to the person that referred it and say thanks again and indicate what happened so he or she knows what the outcome of that case was. This often leads to another referral."

"DON'T underestimate a plain thank-you note. I had a form thank-you letter on the computer, but it still wasn't getting out in a timely fashion. There was always something more important that the staff had to get out. I find handwritten notes are getting much better feedback because people know that they are not some form letter on the computer."

WHEN I get back a nice set of interrogatory answers from some middle manager who stayed up late or worked a weekend to get these responses to me, I write that manager a personal thank-you, and I let her supervisor know what a good job she did for me. I find that this gives me a lot of goodwill in the companies and gives me more business.

USE business social stationery for a more personal touch. This is about 5 x 8 inches and has just the firm name and address without all the lawyers' names. It looks great and personalizes the contact more than regular formal letterhead.

ANOTHER choice for short, personal hand-written notes are informal cards. These are like greeting cards with the fold at the top, blank inside. They come in various sizes, often 5" wide and 4" high when folded (picture a folded piece of business/social stationery). We have our logo embossed on the cover and the firm name and contact information in small print at the bottom of the back cover. The envelopes are imprinted with our return address on the back flap.

STAYING in touch with people—sending thank-you notes, birthday cards, and all types of personalized communication—is very important.

Provide Helpful Information

Be an information broker. Get on a lot of e-mail distribution lists. I receive newsletters from accounting firms, other lawyers, the U.S. Small Business Administration, national industry-specific organizations, and

Encourage every client to let you know what they like— and what they would like different.

local business groups. I don't even know how I got on some of these lists, but I now can speak intelligently on a wide range of topics, which may affect my clients. I may not know all the answers, but at least I have a pretty good idea of the questions.

WHEN you get an RSS feed or Google Alert on a topic of interest to a client, prospect, or referral source, forward it. Being on top of the game is good for your image.

WHEN you have a firm with offices in different states, it is very important to let your clients know you practice in multiple jurisdictions. Many of my clients didn't know we had a practice in New Jersey when they had problems in New Jersey. When I let them know I was the managing partner of our New Jersey office, they were surprised. So, let your clients know. They don't always look at the letterhead, which should list all offices.

Listen

It's important to elicit and listen to client complaints. Client complaints really aren't bad news. Not hearing client complaints is really bad news. Learn how to check in with clients from time to time to just see—particularly if you've delegated work—how's it going. If you discover something is not going right, being able to respond is a very important part of maintaining effective client relations.

DEVELOPING effective and empathetic listening skills is really, *really* critical for lots of reasons. To build effective friendships or effective networks, you must get to know other people, to know what they like and don't like. Learn about their hobbies and their family situations. Let them know you care what's going on with them. Maintaining effective client relations means knowing when the client is happy and knowing when the client is not happy.

Client surveys allow you to obtain feedback about how it's going. Surveys can be in writing, electronic, by telephone, or in face-to-face meetings. Written surveys allow anonymity but may suffer from a low response rate. Consider whether your client base will enjoy or be repelled by such an experience. In the interest of candor, telephone surveys are best when done by someone other than the lawyer who provided the services. A letter in advance confirming the time and outlining the topics to be covered will expedite the process. Client meetings are always valuable, and they convey that you are willing to spend non-billable time making your client happy. However, busy client and lawyer schedules can get in the way. Several Web services exist for surveys via the Internet. The most popular free tool for client surveys may be *www.surveymonkey.com*. Find others by searching "web surveys free." Make sure your survey method allows the client to say what she wants to, rather than just tell you what you think you want to know.

To retain clients, do a client checkup. Check in with clients and ask them if they are satisfied with your services and what needs have not been met.

"Respond *immediately* to client requests. Responsiveness is the single most important reason clients tell us they give our firm repeat business."

When you have reason to believe your client is not happy with your or your firm's performance, be concerned. Ask if there is a problem, and offer to fix it.

T RY to do a postmortem at the end of a matter to get clients' feedback. It may tell why you are not getting more business from them if you are not. You may find out that someone who was working on a matter with them offended them in some way, and it may provide you a way to correct a problem that arose. They may be perfectly happy, and if they are, you want to know that. Try to find out what you did well and what you may not have done so well.

Connecting with the Client

Learn the names of your client's family members. You can inquire about them by name, say hello if you have to call the home. Learn the names of your client's business partners and associates, even if you are representing the client on a personal matter. Make the receptionist, administrative assistant, and secretary your friends.

M AKE house calls. Hardly any lawyers extend to their clients the courtesy of going to their client's office rather having the client come to their office, but it pays off. When you visit the client's place of business, meet the middle managers as well as the officers. Ask for a tour, and meet the people who produce the client's product or perform the services.

M ARKETING requires a whole-firm effort, including staff. If my clients adore my secretary, then I get more business.

If I am down at the courthouse, they will call her about the case because they know her, they like her, and they know she is going to get that message to me. They don't expect me to be in the office every moment of every day or just waiting on their call. When I hire a secretary, one of the first things I say is, "Tell me what your concept of marketing is," and I begin to train that secretary, my paralegals, and my file clerks. I don't care who may come in contact with a client; if they know the whole staff, and they like all of us, then they are comfortable when I am not immediately at the helm.

Negative comments about other lawyers are really counterproductive. That sort of thing never works. It does pay to promote other people, and it pays to promote other lawyers. It pays to promote other lawyers in your firm, and it pays to promote other lawyers on the other side of deals or transactions. But I've never seen it pay to put down competition.

I was at a meeting with a lawyer who sought to impress the client with derogatory remarks about the quality of the representation of the party on the other side. The client never said anything in the course of that conversation, just nodded, but afterward she remarked that she never wanted to do business again with the fellow that I had come in with because she was so offended by that kind of negative commentary.

CALL your clients regularly for no reason at all. Clients appreciate a "no charge" phone call from their lawyer who just wants to check in and say, "Hi, how are you doing?" They may be shocked at first. If you get your clients talking about what's new in their lives, you may uncover a need for legal services of which the client was unaware. Don't think of this as a

sales call, though, as much as a social one: no hard sell! Keep checking in through months of no activity. When that client does need legal services, you'll be there to help.

L ET a client know that you saw her name (favorably) in the news.

D O all you can to make the client feel that he or she is the most important client you have.

Chapter 5

Old Advertising/ New Advertising: Websites and More

What medium will you choose to get your message out? Electronic media have multiplied the options. No one in the twenty-first century can ignore the marketing power of the Internet. Smart rainmakers have figured out how to harness it. Some media are expensive, and some are relatively cheap. Your message can be enhanced or demeaned by the medium. Sending the wrong message in the wrong market can be a costly error, so professional help can be a good investment.

Your Website

Advertising your services starts with your Website. If you haven't reserved your own name as a domain, do so now. Reserve versions of your name—*e.g.*, Deborah, Debra, or Debbie with your last name, maybe ver-

sions with your middle name or initial. How will people look for you? A bare-bones Website is better than no Website, but please, not so bare-bones that it turns people off. Finding that a Website is "under construction" for months at a time sends the wrong message. At the other extreme, bells and whistles that don't work are also a turnoff—literally. Links that go nowhere or to someplace counterintuitive are a no-no.

A MONG many, many other providers, LEXIS/Martindale offers law firm Website design (*www.mgtdesign.com/cws-final*).

F IRM Websites carry their own issues. For example, search for your name on your firm's Website. If there is no result, there's a problem. The firm may have rules about lawyers maintaining their own separate Websites. The bigger your organization, the harder it is to pin down who to talk to about how to elevate your electronic profile while not running afoul of firm rules. Try your technology people, firm marketer, and managing partner. If there's a technology committee, it may be worth your time to try to get on it or at least provide input to the members.

I F you don't have your own professional Website (maybe because the firm doesn't allow it), have your domain name, *www.SuzySmartlawyer.com*, directed to your law firm bio page or LinkedIn profile.

T HE most beautiful Web page is useless if it doesn't come up in your prospective clients' searches. Search engine optimization (SEO) is critical. The file name of your page should include the keywords people are likely to search. A file name of "page one" won't make it happen. A properly programmed Web page will have invisible metatags, which are the keywords seen by search engines. Here are the metatags for the home page of a California lawyer specializing in pharmaceutical product liability:

<meta name="keywords" content="dangerous drug, defective medical device, pharmaceutical liability, doctor, medication, drugs manufacturer, attorney, medical supplements, side effects, lawyer, law firm, personal, injury, Santa Ana, California, Los Angeles, San Diego, Anaheim, Long Beach, Fresno, Bakersfield, Ventura, Orange County, Riverside County, San Bernardino County, LA County, San Diego County, Kern County"/>

D ID you ever wonder why your search history shows a description of some sites as well as the name, or why that description appears at the top of the screen above the URL? It's because a meta description was programmed. This extra can improve your site's visibility.

H ERE is one tipster's view of the minimum Internet requirements for a BtoC (business to consumer) law practice:

- Web page—*e.g.*, *www.lawfirmname.com*, *www.smithjones.com*
- Facebook page
- Desirable bare-bones extras:
  - Blog

If searchers can't find your site, it's the same as if it didn't exist.

◊ Twitter feed
  ◊ Multiple domains that capture likely searches that
  all land on the Website, such as:
  www.JohnSmithattorney.com
  www.WilliamJonesattorney.com
  www.smithjoneslaw.com
  www.smithjones.net
  www.smithandjones.com

Aʟᴡᴀʏs include a description of a picture on your Website.
Search engines can't see pictures, only text.

Mᴀᴋᴇ it easy for Web searchers to contact you by multiple
media. Don't hide your address or phone number—
plenty of people are still wary of transmitting personal information over the ether. Who are the lawyers? Pictures and bios
provide credibility and should be updated regularly. Lack of a
picture for one or more people when the other professionals are
pictured is frustrating. Biographical information that concentrates on law school achievements signals "newbie." If your
lawyers have been published, provide a link to the article if
available electronically or request permission from the publisher
to include a copy as a page on your site.

On the other hand, some women shun publicizing their picture because of fear of harassment—and men in their organization refrain from posting theirs in support.

Hᴏᴡ much text and how much graphic content to include
on a lawyer's Website is a dilemma. Consider what's
important on your page—what are people looking for? If your

firm is housed in an impressive building, a picture could send a message; a picture of your city's skyline . . . maybe not so much. What does a picture of the courthouse add to the viewer's information? Of course you will include your firm's logo. If you include material from other sources, such as government or industry associations, include their logos and maybe a link to their Websites for more information. Videos can be very helpful in conveying information to viewers who don't want to read a lot of text. Do you use accident-simulation or day-in-the-life videos in your practice? Once the case is over, and you edit out personal information, consider adapting such videos to your Website to show the level of work you do.

HOME pages can be simple or complex. Make sure your page can be found readily by search engines. Consider keywords, the most common phrases clients may use to describe your practice. Think like the buyer of those services, not the seller. Make sure your page includes those phrases, preferably multiple times, both obviously and in the programming code known as metatags.

YOUR Internet service provider (ISP) may provide utilities to create a home page without charge. However, you may not like the obscure URL you will be assigned. Having your own domain avoids this problem, and you can program your page to land viewers on your freebie site. Legal directory companies can also help you create a page for a reasonable price. Again, there may be a drawback in having to go through the directory company to get to your page. The most basic home page should allow people to reach you via e-mail.

BEFORE planning your page's content, research many other lawyers' pages. What works? What turns you off? You are sure to get a number of ideas. How will you find a programmer? Sometimes, a programmer's name is on the site. Talk to lawyers who have sites. Ask about what they thought worked well and what they want to do differently. One good thing about your Web page is that you are sure to keep changing it to stay current, so there is plenty of opportunity for improvement.

DON'T get so carried away with your Web page design that it takes forever to load. Web surfers faced with a splash page may leave without clicking to the content. Viewers of a lawyer's Web page are seeking information. Too many graphics or videos slow down the process and could even freeze the user's system—a sure way to alienate your visitors. Make sure all the links actually go somewhere—a "404 Error" message suggests sloppiness.

YOUR site name should be short, easy to spell correctly and easy to remember. The name should clearly relate to your business and include a keyword people are likely to be searching for. Don't be afraid to create multiple domain names which all point to your Website.

ONE theory says that visitors to your site will decide whether to explore it further in the first 30 seconds. Therefore, it is important to show value immediately, such as by offering a free report or service. Content should be important, but not verbose. Include a link to lawyers' biographies and pictures, but not on the landing page; that territory is too dear. Avoid jargon.

B E wary of offers to submit your site to numerous search engines for an inexpensive fee. You may find your site blacklisted, and then no one will be able to find you.

Y OU can provide links to helpful pages for your Web page visitors, and you can also investigate paid or unpaid links from others' Web pages to yours. Include a disclaimer of responsibility for the content of any page other than your own.

Y ES, you think you know if you're getting business from your Website, but maybe not. If new clients simply say they saw you on the Internet, it's hard to know what is and isn't working. On sites you control, include statistics tracking to provide feedback. Others' sites will usually provide you this information for a fee.

S AY a group of people wants to reach out to a lawyer in the middle of the night. As appropriate for your practice area, provide a way for potential clients to do that via your Website, whether it's by e-mail, voicemail, or phone service answered by real person.

W EB hosting has gotten ridiculously cheap. Paying a programmer to create your page can be cheap or expensive. No surprise—you tend to get what you pay for, but that may not be bad. People looking for legal information or a new

The ethical rules for electronic marketing can be especially onerous.

Investigate the rules in the state of your licensure before jumping online.

lawyer are interested in information—*i.e.*, text, rather than fancy graphics. Less can be more.

CHOOSE an appropriate screen name and domain provider. Ideally, you would like to have a screen name with marketing value, such as familylaw@domain.pro. While the number of suffixes has expanded, *.com* remains king. Use it if you can, and consider registering your domain with others as well, such as *.net*. Other possibilities of interest to lawyers are *.pro*, a domain reserved for professionals, *.biz*, and *.info*. Most ISPs allow multiple screen names, so you can have one for business and another for fun. Of course, names such as "hotmama" are not appropriate for business use.

Your Internet Footprint

You have Googled yourself, haven't you? How will you deal with what others see about you if you haven't seen it yourself? You can increase your Web presence on various free lawyer and professional sites such as *www.Martindale.com*, *www.Avvo.com*, *www.Plaxo.com*, *www.Zoom Info.com*, and *www.Spoke.com*. Claim your profile and edit it, but don't feel compelled to complete every field. Information from one site may get picked up on another.

HOW many times a day do you go to Google's home page? But have you ever noticed the link just below the search box, Advertising Programs? Click through to see how you can advertise on Google and also include others' advertisements on your Web page. Learning to use Google AdWords is an art, probably best handled by a professional.

"WE tried AdWords years ago and flushed a lot of money down a rat hole. It has *radically* changed over the years, so we jumped back in a few months ago. It is very, very complicated to do this well. However, we must have finally got it figured out, because traffic to our site has doubled in the last six months. And we are getting business from it, though we find it hard to measure conversion. We know how many people come to the landing pages, but if they go to our Website rather than call (as suggested by the "call to action" on the landing page; we also have a special phone line to ID those callers), they tend to simply say, "I found you on the Internet" or "through Google." Key factors of success are determining the best keywords or phrases, understanding the use of negative keywords, making sure the ad matches the landing page for a high quality score (this is automated by Google), understanding how to bid, and understanding the "tail" theory of keyword marketing, *i.e.*, marketing to many small market niches rather than trying to sell the most popular product or service can result in a greater return.

POTENTIAL clients are looking for lawyers on YouTube. Most of the lawyer videos are talking heads—usually the lawyer or perhaps a testimonial from a grateful client. The description of the video you upload to YouTube should allow viewers to click through to your Website, and the videos there should be available through YouTube. Make sure your video looks professional. Shaky cameras and text misspellings or grammar errors are unlikely to inspire confidence. Your own appearance and demeanor should be professional but not pompous.

PARODIES of lawyer videos available on YouTube demonstrate everything wrong with lawyer videos and commercials. Some lawyer videos pretend to be local to whatever city you included in your search query. Some seem to encourage baseless litigation. Keep yours real.

"YOUTUBE is now the second most used search engine. Its use by lawyers has exploded, but we have just begun to use this technology. It is not a good candidate for DIY, so our firm found a talented videographer from the university. You need a high-quality camera (about $5,000), a green screen, professional lights, and a teleprompter. We filmed about a dozen short FAQ videos on computer forensics—they are already pulling in work, so yes, people really do search YouTube for serious subjects. We also filmed a couple of very-high-tech intros to our company. Most lawyer videos are dreadful: simply a talking head or a talking head with law books behind the person. A good videographer will give you a good video background and even special effects. You don't want to go wild and crazy as a lawyer, but you have to make yourself stand out. Cost will be between $1,000 and $2,000 for a one- to three-minute video (you never want a video to be longer, because folks have short attention spans). However, most videographers will offer you a package deal where, for instance, you get ten one- to two-minute videos for $2,500. Some videographers will have you come to their studio, others will come onsite. The latter tend to be pricier. Doing FAQs relative to your practice area is my best suggestion for lawyers because the title of the video and the tags will contain likely search terms that users are employing."

IF you've got something to crow about, Twitter is the place to tweet it. Make sure your tweets will interest the people you want to follow you. As you certainly know by now, Twitter forces you to be terse—140 characters. How about a pithy comment on the legal issue you are currently working on? "Today I am working on . . ." can get pretty boring, so avoid repetitive use of this lead-in. What if you can't think of what to tweet? Will your clients care about the legislature's bill affecting your practice area? How about court administration? Answer: only if you make it important to your followers' lives. Tweet whenever you have something important, or just interesting, to say—at least once a week. Your Website should allow visitors to easily sign up to follow you on Twitter. Encourage followers to get their acquaintances to follow you, too. You might want to do this on Friday (#FollowFriday is a sort of game where each Friday participants recommend people to follow), although there is nothing wrong with the other days of the week.

MINIMALLY, you must be accessible. Just as consumers expect to be able to locate you in the telephone directory, they expect to be able to find you on the Internet.

YOU can pay for an ad in the church newsletter or for a banner on *www.lawyers.com*. Choose what's right for your practice, your target clientele, your budget. The choices are many, your time—if not resources—probably limited. Choose your advertising efforts with care, and monitor what works. Give it a chance, but don't be stubborn—move on to something else if you are not getting a return on the dollar within a reasonable time.

THE number of Websites channeling work to lawyers seems to increase every day: *www.lexisone.com*, *www.findlaw .com*, *www.attorneyfind.com*, *www.lawyers.com*, *www.lawyer shop.com*, *www.legalmatch.com*, *www.onlineattorneyfinder .com*, *www.gottrouble.com*, etc. The list goes on and on, and these are only some of the general referral lists. Specialty-area organizations also provide electronic lawyer referral, but it's pretty unlikely you are going to get mergers and acquisitions work from a consumer Website, so consider whether any of these sources are right for your practice.

BOOKS about electronic marketing abound. Browse the local bookstore, and check out the ABA Law Practice Management Section bookstore at *www.abanet.org/lpm/publications*.

Legal Directories and Law Lists

Lawyers are well advised to pay attention to their Martindale-Hubbell listing, especially if they are courting business clients. The original rater of attorneys, Martindale-Hubbell (*www.martindale.com*) is changing its rating system. AV has historically been the ratings goal. To achieve a Martindale rating, the lawyer has been required to earn peer review ratings for ethics as well as practice competence. Historically, the V has signified adherence to "general ethical standards." Assuming you pass that hurdle, your abilities were graded: C means legal ability of "good to high," B from "high to very high," and A from "very high to preeminent." A firm has the rating of its highest rated partner.

Under the new system, lawyers will have a numeric rating of 1–5. AV and BV lawyers' ratings will be converted to a number, and for now both ratings will be shown online. The CV rating is being dropped.

Martindale sends out questionnaires on random lists of lawyers to rated lawyers within the same practice area. Questions call for grading legal abilities according to legal knowledge, analytical capabilities, judgment, communication ability, and legal experience. After you have been around a decade or so, hopefully, enough rated lawyers will recognize your name and think well of you for you to obtain a rating. Litigators get out and know more people. It's tougher for lawyers with an office practice.

You can shortcut this process by contacting Martindale-Hubbell at ratings@martindale.com and providing them with a list of people who know your work. This, obviously, is more productive than having your name sent to a bunch of people who have never heard of you.

Plenty of legal directories exist besides Martindale. Many are of lawyers who limit their practice to a specific area, such as Best's *Directory of Recommended Insurance Attorneys* ***http://www3.ambest.com/DPSDirectorySearch/SubHome.aspx?nid=1***. Best's is the bible of the insurance claims industry. Collection agencies farm out business through commercial law lists. Two of the big ones are American Lawyers Quarterly (***www.alqlist.com***) and Forwarders List (***www.forwarderslist.com***). Find out if there is a law list for your practice area.

Some cities support "women's media," such as the women's Yellow Pages. Check the Web to see if there's one in your town. If women small-business owners are your market, this

book will reach them. These books are distributed to corporate buyers who have a mission to assign business to women and minorities.

E-mail and Direct Mail

Beware of solicitations to seek business through "targeted electronic mailings," better known as spam. You've seen it in your inbox, but do you respond? Your prospects are equally likely to be turned off. Many systems will filter out broadcast messages. Spam is subject to numerous restrictions, so be careful with whom you do business. Rather than sending out unsolicited e-mail, a better option is to allow clients and visitors to your Website to subscribe to receive your newsletter and bulletins.

D IRECT mail is not as easy as it looks. One rainmaker reports sending 7,500 pieces to small businesses with no response other than two calls from other lawyers looking for work.

M OST lawyers who have tried direct mail report that it didn't work. The exception to the rule is a lawyer who represents defendants in eviction actions. This lawyer peruses postings in the courthouse and then mails a letter to the allegedly delinquent tenants notifying them of their rights and that his office is available to help.

Traditional Media: Television, Radio, Newspapers and Magazines, Yellow Pages

Think twice before joining a collective television advertising program. The expense is huge, and a lot of the cases are tiny or not meritorious. Not only will you spend a lot of money, but your commitment to the service includes taking the "loss leader" calls, too. The combination can be deleterious to your mental health as well as your pocketbook.

INVESTIGATE collective television advertising, but be careful. This can be very expensive with no guarantee of results. If you proceed, do so in a very focused way. Carefully choose your region and area of practice. A colleague of mine did this, choosing "wrongful terminations." He selected that specialty because the people who ran the service said there were many calls for it and not very many providers. He went in for three months and had maybe eight calls and took four good, solid cases, and he left the service.

CABLE television advertising is more targeted and may be less expensive than the national network station. Advertisements can range from a placard on the community service channel to a half-hour infomercial. Before considering spending any money on these outlets, investigate their demographics. For some practices, such as personal injury or workers' compensation, this type of advertising works well. It is particularly beneficial in targeting foreign-language speakers through advertisements on channels or programs broadcast in their language.

"I KNOW an attorney who has put hundreds of thousands of dollars into advertising through the Lutheran radio stations. What he does is provide information; he will talk about why you need a will, or the three things you need to know when you buy a piece of property or open an escrow account or whatever, and then at the end will say, "Brought to you by . . ." Over a period

No advertising outreach will work unless everyone in the office is aware of the ad and can respond to inquiries appropriately.

of years, he has created this phenomenal niche. He now has five branch offices and a substantial practice. I think that concept can be used by you in your own areas of interest."

WOMEN'S periodicals such as *Today's Chicago Woman* (*www.todayschicagowoman.com*) typically serve urban, upscale, working women. If you are targeting them, this may be a judicious use of your advertising dollars.

ADVERTISING can be effective when done well. Radio, television, and the daily newspaper might come to mind, but these are all very expensive. Don't overlook more targeted publications. Consider a church newsletter or local theater program for your message. Explore specialized ethnic and foreign-language publications.

There are a lot of advantages to using a marketing professional to create and place your ad, not the least of which is an objective eye. This tombstone ad (a bare announcement of a transaction, commonly used to offer initial public offerings of securities) appeared in the weekly business magazine of a major city:

Smith, Jones
is Pleased to Announce
the Expansion of its Pacific Rim Practice
with the Appointment of
Los Angeles Partner
Teresa Manley
and the Opening of its
Hong Kong Office

While one might suspect that Smith, Jones is a law office, it might also be an accounting practice, an investment banking concern, or a marketing company. Nothing in this announcement says to the non-lawyer businessperson reading it what it is Smith, Jones proposes to do for its clients. It would not detract from the dignity of the tombstone one iota for Smith, Jones to describe itself as "Smith, Jones, Attorneys at Law," if indeed that's what it is. The folks at Smith, Jones probably figured they were so well known that they didn't have to clue in anyone not in the know. The benefit of the ad is lost if it fails to communicate enough to attract the attention of the intended audience.

IF you can't afford a display ad in a magazine, see if classified advertising is available instead.

WHEN placing an ad in a periodical, look into buying the 1/3 page size. You are less likely to find yourself sharing space with another ad on the page. This makes your ad more noticeable and memorable.

PERUSE the lawyer advertising in the Yellow Pages for marketing ideas. The biggest ad on the front or back cover may be for a lawyer. Yellow Pages ads still work in the age of Google, obviously more so for some practice areas (criminal, plaintiff personal injury) than others (mergers and acquisitions). On the one hand, ads have gotten more sophisticated. On the other hand, some ads appear to violate the professional responsibility rules. If lawyers are spending this much money year after year, presumably they are seeing a return. As with any other outreach, it depends on how appropriate this medium is for reaching your prospects, how well it is done, and how diligently you pursue it.

BLISS By Harry Bliss

"... Well, I don't know. But if you're not,
you certainly <u>should</u> be Googleable."

Chapter 6

Public Relations:
Press Releases, Brochures, Newsletters, and More

Rainmakers keep their names in the public eye. The art of public relations uses a range of media to get notice of positive information. Communications to various media and the segments of the public those media reach is more challenging than communicating to those who already know you. Content has to be newsworthy as well as help market your services. Electronic press releases can spread your message across the Web at the push of a button, but shooting information into the ether may not be enough to get you noticed.

Press Releases

Press releases are used to submit informational and promotional material to print and electronic media for distribution. All press releases are electronic today. Somebody needs to write the release as in years past,

A fine-tuned public relations campaign is part of your overall marketing effort.

but now SEO-friendly releases include video, pictures, and links to Websites including your firm Website or social media page. In addition, press releases can include invisible metatags—data that will raise the profile of your release in a search result.

WHO should prepare the release? Some possibilities are your marketing person in the law firm and outside PR professionals, or you might do it yourself. Some lawyers believe it takes as much time to work with outside PR professionals as it does to do the job themselves. Also, PR professionals have been known to make some very famous mistakes, ranging from embarrassing typographical errors to trying to justify the unjustifiable (think Enron or AIG.) In a PR piece about using overhead control rather than price increases to increase profit on the same number of sales, a clueless PR professional wrote that with proper overhead control a business didn't need to make any sales to produce profit.

Distribution services will send your piece to many outlets at once. Not only is the publicity itself good marketing, but each electronic outlet results in an inbound link, thereby enhancing SEO (search engine optimization). In choosing a service, investigate to whom they distribute. Ideally, you want old media outlets as well as Internet postings. Business lawyers will want to include industry publications, both paper and electronic. All lawyers will want to make sure to hit niche publications and sites likely to reach the target audience. An electronic service can also work with you to include metatags to optimize your search engine visibility.

YOU can also send releases by e-mail to your personal media outlet list. You can do this as your exclusive distribution system or complement an electronic distribution by sending to personalized, smaller outlets.

Wide distribution will certainly include the major dailies in your community and major business or industry publications. A supplementary distribution might go to neighborhood papers, local legal publications, and publications of organizations to which you belong. Personalize the piece for the recipient if at all possible. Identify the section where this information should go. If it is going to your alumni news, include the year you graduated and the school or the college. If it's going to your neighborhood paper, make sure you indicate that you're a resident of that neighborhood. In a big city, there are lots of neighborhood niche outlets.

MANY Websites provide free information on creating press releases, useful even if you are not doing them yourself. Promoting yourself along with your firm is easier if you build a working relationship with your law firm's marketer. Help her, and she is likely to make herself available to help you.

ABROAD distribution news release should be used for information that is truly newsworthy. That could include the decision on a big case or a major appointment or award. More prosaic news may be most economically communicated via Twitter or LinkedIn.

When you're talking about press releases, you're really talking about two things: the release itself and distribution to your media outlet list— who is going to get the press release?

The Writing

Everything else is useless if the release is not well written. It has to look like news of interest to the readers of that medium. Avoid lawyerese! You need keywords—those popular words and phrases people are searching for on the Internet. Use the same words too repeatedly, though, and your release will get electronically passed over as search-engine spam. Repetitive use of the same phrase doesn't make for good copy once people do get to the text.

Here's a guide for keyword density:

Headline: main keyword should not appear in more than 15% to 20% of all words in the headline

Summary: main keyword should not appear in more than 2% to 10% of all words in the summary

Body: main keyword should not appear in more than 3% to 5% of all words in the body

D ON'T know the keywords related to your area? Sites such as ***www.wordstream.com*** can help.

W RITE in active, not passive, voice. In the first paragraph, identify who, what, when, where, and why. That may be the only paragraph that is going to be picked up by third-party sites and publishers. Include a quote for interest, and lead with the point you want to emphasize. Include links if appropriate.

A RELEASE can be written with several different leads, depending on the facet you want emphasized. For example, for a seminar, the lead could be the sponsoring organization, the seminar topic, or a featured speaker. Don't be afraid to mention competitors, if appropriate. If the list of speakers at a seminar you want to promote includes lawyers from other major firms, go ahead and use the firm name. Web surfers searching for that firm's name will find your release that promotes you.

Quote. Use direct quotes whenever possible. A good quote can make a routine story unique.

Be accurate. Be sure all your facts are absolutely true. Excessive use of adjectives, puffery, or exaggeration can lead to irreparable damage.

Grammar. Check your release for correct punctuation and spelling. Spell check is not sufficient.

Contact. Show the contact name, e-mail, and direct-dial phone number.

Format. Bold, italics, bullets, and subheads can make the page easier to read and enhance SEO.

Get their attention with a headline. Getting your release noticed among the river of communications created on any day requires a clean and catchy headline.

Include a summary. Describe the release in a sentence. Avoid filler words. Be terse.

Add photos and graphics. Action photos are ideal, but minimally include your picture, and describe the picture. Include your firm logo if you have one. Every rainmaker should have a "publicity still"—a head shot taken by a professional photographer for your Website and other PR. A plain background is fine, although some lawyers like to be photographed in front of their law library. Some photographers who specialize in professional portraits, in fact, have a "library" backdrop. Photos tend to come in categories: the lineup, the handoff, the handshake, the ribbon cut, etc. Editors really prefer interesting photos if at all possible. Important for women rainmakers is controlling the photo—you want to avoid the cleavage or gam shot. Even if the medium has its own photographer, try to persuade your contact to use the photo you know shows you to best advantage.

End. Mark the end with ### or -30- (the traditional ways to signify the end of a reporter's copy.)

Sending it off. E-mail press releases in MS Word. You can send your document as an attachment to your message, which may be the best way to save formatting. On the other hand, pasting the release into the body of your message may be more likely to get it read. Do not send uneditable PDFs. If you make your release uneditable, it cannot be incorporated into the target medium. Editors want to edit, and your release must be conformed to the medium's format.

YES, you can hire a company like Business Wire (*www.businesswire.com*; 888/381-9473) or Press Release Network (*www.pressreleasenetwork.com*) to distribute your press release to selected media throughout the country. But if you really want some attention, make sure your distributor can provide SEO service. Each service maintains various targeted distribution lists. Cost depends on how many lists you choose. Many new distributors have come on the scene for distribution solely to electronic media. A professional service allows you to reach many more outlets, and you have saved the time and effort otherwise necessary to research and create an accurate distribution list.

M ANY companies, such as *www.Prlog.org*, *www.online prnews.com*, and *www.free-press-release.com*, offer free basic electronic press release distribution.

These sites include instruction on how to write a press release and offer upgraded services for a fee, as well.

H ERE is an actual PRlog press release with my notes italicized and underlined:

Headline:

Teddy Snyder to Speak at
2010 Council on Litigation Management Conference

Summary:

Teddy Snyder, Attorney/Structured Settlement Consultant at Ringler Associates, has been selected to speak at the 2010 Annual Conference of the Council on Litigation Management (CLM).

Always include this phrase, unless there is some reason to hold the release:

FOR IMMEDIATE RELEASE

Note date and place of release

PR Log (Press Release)—January 06, 2010—New York, NY—(PR.COM)—01/XX/10—Teddy Snyder, Attorney/Structured Settlement Consultant at Ringler Associates, has been selected to speak at the 2010 Annual Conference of the Council on Litigation Management (CLM). Ms. Snyder is slated to speak on the topic "Defending a Damages Claim."

The conference will be one of the largest fully inclusive defense industry conferences convened in 2010. It will be held March 24–26 in Ponte Vedra, Florida, and will feature approximately 150 speakers. The conference is expected to draw attendees from around the world. Registration is now open at ***www.litmgmt.org/annual-conference***.

Teddy (Theda) Snyder, Esq., CSSC, is an attorney and Certified Structured Settlement Consultant in the Beverly Hills, California, office of Ringler Associates. Ringler Associates is the oldest and largest structured settlement company. Teddy joined Ringler in 2001 after more than twenty years of litigation and litigation management experience, including more than one hundred trials.

She has presented lectures to numerous legal organizations, state bar associations, and annual meetings of the American Bar Association. Her articles have been published in a variety of legal and insurance journals and newspapers, and she has written three books about running a law practice, all published by the American Bar Association.

About the Council on Litigation Management

The Council is a nonpartisan alliance of thousands of insurance companies, corporations, general counsel, risk managers, claims adjusters, and attorneys. Through education and collaboration, its goals are to create a common interest in the representation by firms of companies and to promote and further the highest standards of litigation management in pursuit of client defense. To learn more about the Council, please visit *www.litmgmt.org*, or contact Adam Potter.

# # #

Contact information and tags:

E-mail Contact	: <u>Click to e-mail</u> (sydney.posner@litmgmt.org)
Issued By	: Sydney Posner
Phone	: 9545620539
Address	: 2166 Broadway, Suite 14F
Zip	: 10024
City/Town	: New York
State/Province	: New York
Country	: United States
Categories	: Legal, Insurance
Tags	: litigation, litigation/management
Last Updated	: Jan 06, 2010
Shortcut	: *http://prlog.org/10477552*

A PRESS release posted on a social media site needs extra oomph to get noticed. Font size, color, and effects inappropriate for submission to print media are de rigueur for catching the eye of the casual reader scanning the posts.

ADVERTISING is something you pay for; publicity is something you beg for. A stream of positive publicity familiarizes the public—and the media—with your name. Even if everything you send to a source doesn't get used, the familiarity created by a communication stream makes it more likely that the most important stories will. Committee appointments, speaking

engagements, and publication of articles in other media can all be the subject of a press release for the right outlet. Let people know you are proud of the new lawyer in your office or that your upgraded technology now provides new client benefits. People remember the name of the lawyer they heard from last.

Having your name appear repeatedly in the media can bring you respect. One rainmaker who successfully publicized one of her speaking engagements reports receiving this comment: "I saw the announcement of your speech. I knew you were a lawyer, and I knew you did civil litigation, but I didn't realize you practiced in this area." The more people see your name, the more they're likely to remember you when it comes time for representation, even if it's only to call you up and ask you for a referral to somebody else—a wonderful way to build business networks, by the way.

A good public relations program never stops, but publicity professionals disagree on how often to issue press releases. One theory has it that you must continually bombard the media with, it is hoped, newsworthy information so the recipient is familiar with your name. The opposing view states that too many releases about minor events is like crying wolf—when the really important event is publicized, you will be overlooked. Presumably there is a happy medium.

Because publicity is packaged as news, the information carries with it the implied endorsement of the medium. Some publications, such as neighborhood papers and your alumni news, may reprint just about any press release. Others may be quite difficult to crack. Keep trying. By the time an editor has seen your name on the fourth or fifth release, he or she may be convinced you're someone special, who readers should know about.

Using a PR Professional

Consider hiring a public relations consultant to help you choose a target market, fashion a consistent image, and execute a marketing plan. Count on six to twelve months before seeing results.

GET *appropriate* help. For example, are you interested primarily in creating a brochure? If so, you may need someone with great visual skills and a handsome portfolio of artwork. If you need to better define your niche in the market, research skills are important. If you don't want print or television ads, be wary of someone who stresses those skills in the interview. Ask about other similar work the PR professional has done. Review samples of other product to see if it suits your taste. Make sure that you're on the same wavelength. Using a PR professional doesn't eliminate your time commitment to getting the job done. Getting the job done is not cheap if you want it done right.

If you have never done your own public relations and are not feeling particularly bold, hire a PR professional for a limited time and learn everything you can.

CONTACT the communications or journalism department of your local college or university to inquire about bringing a public relations intern on board for free or inexpensive assis-

tance. Alternatively, get together with another business owner and jointly hire a new grad, each of you taking responsibility for half the employee's time and compensation.

R ETHINK the public relations value of your cases and community activities. You may be more newsworthy than you realize. Sensitize all your lawyers to the public relations value of their cases and community activities. Create a procedure for in-house use for lawyers to report speeches, board appointments, and awards to your PR person.

Brochures

A firm brochure may be your first contact with a potential client. Some rainmakers swear that the best brochure for small and medium organizations is an $8^1/_2$ x 11–inch trifold or $8^1/_2$ x 14–inch fourfold piece. Hire a professional, or do it yourself with brochure templates readily available on the Web.

M AKE your firm brochure focused, efficient, and cost effective. One option is to use pocket portfolios. Choose portfolios with die cuts to insert a business card. Put only information that won't change—like your firm name and logo—on the most expensive element—*e.g.*, the glossy folder. You can purchase printed folders or stickers for placing on plain folders. Firm description, attorney bios, and practice areas can appear on separate pages. Stair-step the heights so the title of each page is visible. Customize content for the recipient. For example, only include descriptions of the practice areas and department personnel relevant to that client's needs.

" A LWAYS send a thank-you letter or handwritten note to a lawyer who refers a client, enclosing several business cards and a firm brochure. Cost to marketing budget: a first-class postage stamp. An out-of-state lawyer recently referred a major PI case to me as the direct result of receiving our brochure, resulting in a six-figure fee."

Newsletters

Newsletters are a tried-and-true way to communicate with current and potential clients. Yours can be electronic or sent by mail. Ask clients which they prefer. You can send information blasts electronically and longer newsletters by mail. Make sure your newsletter is helpful, not just a trumpeting of your own achievements. You need not be wedded to a burdensome publication schedule. One woman rainmaker who specializes in adoption sends out an annual wrap-up in January.

Send "bulletins" to clients about new developments as they occur. You can e-mail clients who opt-in to this service, but clients may be most likely to retain a hard-copy piece.

C ONSTANT Contact (*www.constantcontact.com*) and MyEmma (*www.myemma.com*) let you send e-mail newsletters to distribution lists for a modest price.

" W E use Constant Contact to send our monthly electronic newsletter. The cost varies per month from $15 for up to 500 addresses to $150 for up to 25,000 addresses. This is for permission-based e-mail only. Their deliverability rate is consistently over 97 percent, and you can track your results. We also use Constant Contact to send out electronic discovery news

SAMPLE CONSTANT CONTACT NEWSLETTER

RINGLER
structured settlement services
BEVERLY HILLS
888-734-3910 *toll free*

TEDDY SNYDER, ESQ. CSSC

A Certified Structured Settlement Consultant, and licensed attorney, Teddy has over 25 years of experience in structures and the law. She brings a unique perspective and creativity to designing, presenting and negotiating settlement annuity plans for injured parties. Teddy's litigation experience includes more than 100 trials.

52%

of cases structured by
RINGLER ASSOCIATES
are less than $50,000.

Since 1975, brokers from
RINGLER ASSOCIATES
have structured over
157,000 cases.

LexisNexis
Workers' Compensation
Law Center

Teddy Snyder

Workers' Compensation
Notable Person 2008

Update *from the Beverly Hills office*

YEAR-END ALERT: Avoid New Reporting Law

Close Out Medicare Beneficiaries' Claims by December 31, 2009 and Avoid the New Reporting Law

CMS

Settlements, judgments, payments and awards to Medicare beneficiaries after January 1, 2010 are subject to new reporting requirements.

To avoid this extra task, the claim must be completely closed out by year-end 2009. For liability claims, this means complete close-down of the claim through payments of a lump sum or structured settlement premium. For workers' compensation claims, it means a lump sum or structured settlement payment which closes out the claimant's medical claim.

The new electronic reporting law enhances Medicare's ability to enforce the Secondary Payer Law against both Medicare beneficiaries and primary payers (insurance carriers and self-insureds.)

For Medicare beneficiaries' claims which remain open after January 1, 2010, please contact me for assistance in evaluating the claim and no later than when you are ready to make an offer to conclude the claim. We can help you put together a plan which complies with the Medicare Secondary Payer Law and gets your case settled.

e-mail Teddy
Teddy's bio
CMS

Since 1975, RINGLER brokers have provided the finest structured settlement services to injured parties, placing over 157,000 structures with payments that are guaranteed and tax free or tax deferred.

Sincerely,

RINGLER ASSOCIATES
STRUCTURED SETTLEMENT SERVICES

TEDDY SNYDER, Esq., CSSC
Certified Structured Settlement Consultant
TSnyder@ringlerassociates.com
888-734-3910 *toll free*
310-461-3550 *direct*
866-691-5252 *fax*
"WHY RINGLER?"

alerts to attorneys with whom we have a relationship. We used to send out such e-mails ourselves and consistently had a problem with spam filters. Constant Contact has a very good relationship with spam filter vendors and, as they are known to be permission based, their e-mails are rarely trapped. This is a fantastic marketing tool at a reasonable price. They also offer a sixty-day free trial."

One of the benefits of these services is mailing list management. You get a report of how many people opened the e-mail, what links were clicked, what the invalid addresses are, and who is opting out. Allowing opt-outs is professional and avoids ill will.

Event Publicity

Take a booth at a trade show. If your firm concentrates on serving a particular industry, investigate whether there is a convention where you could showcase your services. If elder law is your specialty, investigate shows serving that demographic segment. Have plenty of informational material available and informed staff at the booth. Invite browsers to throw their business cards or a registration slip into a large fishbowl to win a prize. Make the prize fun: a piece of luggage or briefcase or perhaps a getaway weekend, *not* a technical book or "free consultation." Giveaways without practical value can be a waste of money. A pen may be retained, at least for a while, but chances are your prospect doesn't need a rubber squeezy globe.

HAVE your firm co-sponsor a major charity event. The cost is often surprisingly small. If high-worth individuals—or their businesses—are your target market, this is an excellent way to enter that market with a favorable glow about you.

Always respond promptly to calls from the media.

Publicity is cumulative.

Potential clients need to hear your name and receive your message multiple times before it registers.

Media Relations

Get to know the reporters in your community—especially the ones who cover the legal or business beat. Feed them stories and information that they would not otherwise uncover or understand. Be the reporter's best resource.

D O you think your expertise would make great talk show fodder? For a small sum, you can list your expertise with the National Talk Show Guest Registry (*www.talkshowregistry.com*). Or you can try to communicate directly with the talent coordinator of the show that interests you (people on the set who will be televised are collectively referred to as "talent"). This works best if you are presenting a package of several people who can address the topic.

S END a letter to the editor. A well-written letter can have surprising results. Other magazines may call to follow up. You can publicize your views and earn favorable personal publicity at the same time. This is one way to keep your name in the public eye in your community.

W HEN you want to get a story into the news, pitching it by phone and e-mail directly to a name in the medium may be better than merely broadcasting a press release. This can be a stand-alone outreach or a follow-up to a press release. If it is a follow-up, you will need to demonstrate how this medium will benefit from additional, exclusive information. Assuming you can get a response, this allows you to make a connection and respond to concerns. Even if you are rejected this time, try to get information to learn what they are looking for so the next effort is successful. Ask what types of stories they are looking for, how else you can help them. Take the opportunity to make small conversation, ask for alternate phone numbers or e-mail addresses, or ask them out for lunch. A friendly encounter today may result in getting the next pitch picked up.

Chapter 7

Writing and Speaking

Opportunities abound for disseminating your ideas and raising your profile. Finding places to publish your work on the Internet is not the problem—turning it into revenue is.

The most prestigious opportunities remain with traditional bar and CLE organizations. Every book on marketing counsels lawyers to write and speak to attain prominence, yet nobody says how to get the gig! CLE organizations are inundated with volunteers' requests for a podium. Lay groups are difficult to identify and even harder to reach. What's the answer?

Speaking and writing bootstrap each other. The first slot is often the hardest to get. Web publications help, but not as much as writing an article for a print medium. It can be in a scholarly law review or a more accessible legal magazine. Write on the area in which you want to make rain.

Writing

Your own Web page, a site you can control, is the first place you will want to post content. Your blog deserves pride of place. Unlike Twitter or LinkedIn updates, this online journal offers you unlimited space to record your thoughts, observations, and advice. Start with a headline and date. Write content that is pertinent to why people are visiting your site in the first place. Keep it brief, and include pictures or links as appropriate. Use words that match the searches your potential clients are likely to use. Explore programming metatags into your blog page to increase its visibility.

NUMEROUS providers, such as *www.LiveJournal.com*, *www.Blogger.com*, *www.WordPress.com*, *www.typepad.com*, and *www.Xanga.com*, will host your blog for free or a small monthly charge. When you choose one of these options, the URL or Web address includes the name of the provider. So, in my case, "Free California MCLE" became *www.freecalifornia-mcle.blogspot.com*. Monica Bay is the popular editor of *Law Technology News*. Her blog, The Common Scold is found at *http://commonscold.typepad.com*. Some providers may include advertising, over which you lack control. You could end up with content from a competitor or other incompatible business next to your own.

SOMETIMES you can send a pitch or query letter to the publication asking if it is interested in a certain type of article. A negative response can save a lot of work. A positive response will generally provide length and style guidelines. Again, being able to write to the publisher's specifications the first time is the most efficient way to proceed. However, most publications will not commit without seeing the finished article.

DON'T hesitate to publish in a newsletter or local bar publication, even if you really seek a wider audience. Many national publications, such as ABA magazines, regularly review local bar publications and solicit revision for a national audience.

Offer to write a client's newsletter or conduct a seminar for its customers.

If you just want to shape the discourse, consider writing a Wikipedia article. You won't get any credit, but you do create the outline for the changes that follow. You can also use this "objective" reference in marketing materials. Subsequent authors' changes can be frustrating, though. I created an article on structured sales, in part because I wanted to create a link from the article on Tax Code section 1031 like-kind exchanges to the structured sale article. Then one of my competitors took it out. I talked to him about it later, and he didn't understand that our potential clients wouldn't search for something they didn't know about—they had to be led. Eventually, someone put the link back in.

R ECYCLE your legal memoranda and briefs into publishable articles. Then recycle the article with minor changes for different publications and for posting on your Website. This gives you maximum exposure for the same work. Naturally you want to reach totally distinct audiences. You may be able to rework course materials written to accompany a lecture for a law review article and then revise again for a lay audience industry publication.

B E alert to specialty publications for your target market. Virtually every category of professionals is served by a specialty periodical. The problem is all the lawyers who are already pitching articles to it. To stand out from the crowd, try writing on a new angle.

Keep your eyes open for newcomers to the periodical market, many of which are Web-based. One recent example is *Sue* magazine (***www.magazinenamedsue.com***), a publication for women in litigation. Read industry "what's happening" columns, which might announce a

new publication. When you see that announcement, act fast. Write a sample article and pitch it to the publisher. Right now he or she is probably more worried about advertisers than writers. Providing Web-ready copy is a blessing to the harried publisher. On the other hand, if you "write like a lawyer"—*i.e.*, in redundant, lengthy sentences—forget getting published at all. No publisher will commit editing time to shape your article so you can get the PR benefit.

IN tough economic times, pay-to-play can get your article published. You agree to advertise in the publication, and they publish your article. The article still has to meet their publication standards. Presumably this is a publication where your firm would like to advertise—otherwise, why are you writing for it? Because there is so much you can do with a copy of your published article, a deal like this may be worthwhile and an ideal way to reach your coveted demographic. The delicate negotiation may be best handled by someone other than the lawyer who will write the article, such as your law firm's marketer.

THERE are many ways to publicize your speeches and recently published articles. You can announce them with a tweet (on Twitter) or on your profile page on social media sites. You can submit speech dates to calendars at legal periodicals or at sites like *www.InsideLegal.com*. If your article is available online, send contacts the link with a note saying something like, "In case you missed this . . ." If the article is not available to the public, check with the publisher to confirm your copyright status. Minimally, you should be able to distribute copies in limited fashion, which would constitute fair use (depending on the circumstances). Usually this means that sending out a limited number

of copies directly to contacts may be acceptable, but posting the article on your Website probably would be forbidden.

Keep writing. As new developments occur in your area, write an article. If you look over the periodicals you receive, you will see many articles are descriptive rather than analytical. Once you get the hang of it, descriptive articles that alert readers to a new development are really rather easy to churn out. Be first.

Speaking

Once you are known as an expert on a subject from your writings, you are likely to get invited to speak. Knowing when to turn down a speaking offer is difficult. You want to reach your target audience, yet, especially in the beginning of your marketing program, any exposure is helpful. Practice never hurts either.

AT some point you will find you are speaking so often that you lack adequate time for lawyering. Measure the rainmaking effectiveness of your speaking engagements and adjust as necessary.

ALWAYS bring your own short introduction, which can be read verbatim by the host or moderator. Otherwise you may find you have lost some of the public relations value of giving the speech. The introduction should tell the audience about how you help people with problems just like theirs (presumably the issue you are about to discuss). This is the time to lavish praise on yourself, since it will look as if it is coming from the moderator. However, a humorous, modest acknowledgment can break the ice with your audience:

Never leave them without a handout with your name, address, e-mail, and phone number on it.

Write your own speeches and publish. Take credit for what you've done.

💧 "Thanks, Henry. You read that just the way I wrote it."

💧 "Thanks, Henry. Of all the introductions I've ever had, yours was the most recent."

A light tone is fine, but unless you are very adept at humor, avoid telling jokes as part of a professional presentation. When stony silence results, there is no graceful exit.

❝ I STARTED marketing by teaching at a local law school. It had an extension program, and I gave an estate planning course for six women from Pasadena. Three of them became clients, and one of them is still a major client. I would speak for YMCAs. I would speak for any group that wanted something in my field. I don't do that anymore, because it doesn't sufficiently cull out the clients that I'm trying to attract from those that I cannot serve well. But early in my career I was starting from nothing, and I was trying to build a client base. It worked."

❝ I LIKE to teach, so it's natural that I have served on the advisory boards of the USC Probate and Trust Conference and on the UCLA Probate Institute. By sitting on those advisory boards I'm making myself known to the other lawyers on the board, many of whom are from larger firms, and large firms have conflicts and need you at times. Because I'm a solo, I'm not perceived as a problem for the referring sources. I am not going to take other business from them. They know that they can refer this business to me and I will not take other matters."

M ARKET yourself to organizations that might be interested in sponsoring a seminar on your area of expertise with you as the featured speaker. Working with an established organ-

ization avoids the expenses of a self-sponsored seminar and lends credibility. Don't expect an honorarium, but you can expect to attract new clients.

Put on a series of seminars in your office. Hire a PR professional to brainstorm with you on the title, write the press release, and create a media outlet list.

Webinars have advantages and disadvantages. People from a wide geographic area—the whole world, really—can attend your seminar. It is convenient; they can attend from their computer at home, at work, or at Starbucks. The cost to sponsor is small compared to renting a hall and providing food and drink. The Webinar can be recorded and made available on your Website either for the public or for people you have provided with an access code. On the other hand, Webinar attendees are likely to be distracted. They may switch to other applications, do other work, or step away from the computer. In some Webinar applications, attendees see a PowerPoint or similar graphic presentation and hear the presenters. This is not as visually stimulating as a live presentation. Other Webinar applications allow a split screen, and a camera can provide a visual of the speaker. There is a danger that the speaker will move out of the camera's range and present a blank screen to the audience. Another disadvantage is that there is no visual feedback for the speaker to gauge if the viewers are following the presentation. Do they look puzzled? Struggling to keep up? No way to tell. Webinars are appropriate for business clients with ready access to high-speed computers. At the other end of the scale, for attorneys trying to establish a bond with local consumer clients,

Let your referral sources know when you're speaking or when an article you've written has come out.

If your local bar association does not have a speakers' bureau, volunteer to form one. You will be at the top of the list when inquirers request a speaker.

The most coveted speaking engagements are on radio and television shows.

Consider putting together a promotional DVD that shows what a fascinating speaker you are on some riveting topic.

live contact is probably preferable. There is a broad range in between, and both types of seminars have their place, especially if the sponsor is a CLE or industry organization.

Regardless of who is the sponsor, try to get a DVD of your presentation, which you can then distribute to clients and prospects. ***www.AttorneyCredits.com*** is always on the lookout for good material for their Continuing Legal Education programs. They handle the technical side, and the speaker is co-owner of the copyright.

ARRANGE a graphic for your DVD. One financial marketing expert says that sending the right DVD package is impressive enough, so much so that a significant number of recipients will contact you without ever playing it.

A newcomer to the audio-only industry is ***www.AccessMCLE.com***. If you have a pre-packaged program, they may be interested in talking to you.

" I SUGGEST giving a seminar for lawyers who practice outside your area of expertise about how two areas of law interrelate. I recently gave a seminar on the interplay of bankruptcy and family law. The domestic practitioners were unfamiliar and apparently uncomfortable with the issues. As a result, I have received several referrals. In addition, I now represent four of the attendees in disputes with their own clients."

D ON'T speak exclusively at CLE events. Rather, speak to the potential clients themselves. Reach them through targeted trade associations.

O FFER to e-mail a special handout to audience members. Your subsequent e-mail will allow them to easily save your contact information. You can add their e-mail addresses to your database for e-mails, newsletters, and holiday cards.

W HY do some lawyers get asked to speak again and again, while for others it's a one-time event? Of course, some lawyers have unique expertise, but in many cases it's because the lawyer has a reputation not only of being an excellent presenter but also someone who follows instructions and makes the sponsor's life easy. Here are some hints for being asked back time and again:

◆ Make sure you understand your assignment. There is nothing worse than a speaker who shows up just in time

Offer to speak gratis in-house to select businesses.

for her presentation, only to give the same speech that someone else gave earlier. The converse happens when the program brochure has promised coverage of a specific subject and no one mentions it.

- Speak in a natural way. *Don't read prepared text.* If you are using a lapel microphone (lavaliere), don't turn your head away from it. Never start by apologizing for the program or text or stating that everything you are about to say is in the materials. Speak for your allotted period of time. Running long is rude to the audience and the speakers who follow you. Don't judge the audience's interest in the other speakers. Have a good conclusion—don't state, "That's all I have to say."

- Understand your audience. Adult learners want their instructors to be interesting and entertaining, but their primary desire is for practical, down-to-earth suggestions of immediate value in the area covered by the course. While a humorous tone is fine, avoid wasting the audience's time with "warm-up" jokes; get to the point right away. Lawyers attend courses to become better lawyers and to make more money.

- Follow the sponsor's format requirements for course materials and get them in on time. Find out if the sponsor intends to reprint the materials as an article, as this will dictate style—*e.g.*, text vs. outline.

- Make sure that your materials convey meaningful information, not just a list of topics. People who did not attend the lecture as well as audience members should be able to use your materials as a resource in the future.

- Understand that at least 65 percent of your message is conveyed by means other than the words you speak. Your appearance, body language, hand gestures, and tone of voice all communicate a message that can detract from or belie your words.
- People learn the most when they both hear and see the message. Use computer graphics to emphasize your points and bring the audience along as you speak.
- Use your course materials for the big picture. Cover only the highlights in your talk. Make sure any case citations are in the materials. If a case has just come out and you must give a citation, project it on screen. As a last resort, state the citation twice to make sure everyone gets it.

Keep your curriculum vitae current. You never know when you will need to produce it in a hurry. *Take a PowerPoint course.*

" I THINK the easiest way to get a speaking engagement with a non-lawyer organization is to find out who the executive director is—they all have executive directors. If you are reviewing the community college brochure, and you see that somebody is teaching an adult education course in the area where you practice, you may want to contact the person giving that course and offer to speak as a guest lecturer. I think you have to select these groups carefully to be sure the demographics conform to what you are trying to achieve. All of these groups have their professional associations. A targeted Web search will ferret them out. Again, you are going to have to make a personal connection—e-mail and call the person, take them out, let them get to know you personally. These organizations always want speakers, and as long as you have identified an appropriate group, that makes sense in terms of use of your time."

Women's organizations typically have a preference for women speakers. Especially for a novice public speaker, women's groups offer a friendly, more accessible podium.

V OLUNTEER to speak to school classes. This is a good way to connect with the parents and the faculty. High school students may be in the market for a lawyer sooner than you might imagine.

S PEAK to other law firms about how they can utilize your specialty services. Consider a presentation title: "What Every ___ Lawyer Needs to Know about ___ Law." For example, if you are a tax specialist seeking referrals, perhaps you could speak on "What Every Employment Litigator Needs to Know about Tax Law." You will increase your desirability as a speaker if you are also a certified CLE provider.

Chapter 8

Gifts and Entertainment

Entertaining clients and giving gifts can mean walking a narrow line. Your choices will be governed by the nature of your practice and your clients.

Gifts

While it might seem logical to spend more money on the bigger clients, many corporations have rules forbidding employees to accept gifts or entertainment worth more than a nominal amount. It's perfectly acceptable to inquire if such a policy is in place before sending tickets or a gift that the recipient will only have to return.

Gift cards—they're always the right size, says one rainmaker. Gift cards for a variety of stores are readily available—even at the supermarket. Starbuck's cards seem to be the most in demand. Cards for iTunes are also popular. If you have a consumer practice, gift cards for the supermarket itself will be welcomed—and can make a difference to your client's holiday festivities.

WE give fruit baskets to high-dollar referral sources. Depending on their work situation, I might ask for a home address.

HAVE you heard of the Bar and Grill singers? I give their CDs to lawyers at holiday time. This is a group of Austin, Texas, lawyers who sing about a lawyer's life to the tune of pop hits. You can hear one of their best songs on YouTube (*http://www.youtube.com/watch?v=5TkuZ5oI9uY*). Their CDs are guaranteed to get a lawyer or someone who works with lawyers laughing in their car or on the bus during the morning commute.

The advertising specialty industry can put your firm name and logo on pretty much anything—but consider what is most appropriate for your recipients. And please try to be a little imaginative. Giving someone yet another coffee mug or duffel bag may not be appreciated. I received four commuter cups one year from our various vendors.

IF your intended recipient is a golfer, there is no better gift than golf balls. The need is unquenchable.

Gift giving runs the gamut from homemade desserts to advertising specialty items bought by the dozen to expensive designer items. The gifts you choose for clients greatly depend on the nature of your practice.

"I LIKE gifts that are somewhat personal. For instance, a surprising—well, maybe not—number of my clients are feminists, and I give away lots of copies of Mary Catherine Bate-

son's *Composing a Life*, Clarissa Pinkola Estes' *Women Who Run with the Wolves*, and John Gray's *Men Are from Mars and Women Are from Venus*. Of course, choosing an appropriate gift depends on the recipient."

E VEN today, a gift from a woman to a man can be taken for something other than a business gesture. Avoid gifts that suggest intimacy. Books, elegant office supplies, or luggage are fine; boxer shorts with red hearts at Valentine's Day are not.

"I GIVE my clients homemade cakes on birthdays, candy corn at Halloween, and seasonal goodies for the holidays."

"I GIVE houseplants or fancy food baskets at holiday time and for birthdays. I seem to be on the mailing list for every catalog in the world, including those for fancy fruits, gourmet meats, and every variety of delicacy wrapped in tinted plastic in an elaborate basket."

U SING the Internet to choose gifts can solve a number of problems—most notably shipping and saving time. You can also find some great gift ideas and bargains. Looking for a gift for a client recently transferred to a cold climate, I checked out winter wear at *www.Landsend.com* and *www.REI.com* before deciding on a pair of glomitts (a cross between gloves and mittens.) I had originally chosen a balaclava (a detached hood), but even the Website was out of stock on the size I needed. Imagine if I had wasted my time going to the store!

Send clients poinsettia plants at Christmas.

THE best gift is one that brings the giver to mind every time the recipient uses it. Therefore, the gift should be something that the client will value and use often. I have sent credit card calculators with a likeness of my business card engraved on the back.

EVEN expensive junk is junk. I'd rather have a Starbucks gift certificate than a silver-plated hourglass engraved with the giver's company name, and I would have more goodwill toward the giver.

I LOSE pens. I don't know where they go. I go through them like popcorn. Finally, I figured that if I was leaving pens all over town, maybe my clients were, too, so the pens may as well have some marketing value. Now I order pens in quantities of three hundred. My name, firm name, address, phone, and e-mail are on the barrel.

SHY away from gag gifts. Did you read about the firm that sent out fake hand grenades—and their clients who called in the bomb squads?

Entertaining

Many lawyers find the golf course or tennis court an excellent place to entertain clients. Many companies make golf events part of their corporate culture. Some women rainmakers advise talking golf lessons so you won't be excluded from these important outings. One sponsored a seminar for other women lawyers on the etiquette of various sports, teams, and betting.

Another school of thought advises to pick things *you* like to do when entertaining clients. There's no sense pretending to like football if you don't know a blitz from a safety. Clients will pick up on your genuine enthusiasm or disinterest. It's okay to invite men to a ballet or opera.

Another rainmaker reports, "I like to bring clients to political and charitable events if I know the person well enough to know I'm not going to create stress."

Tickets to blockbuster museum shows can be scarce. If you are a museum member, you will have early notice and opportunity to purchase these tickets. Invite your client or referral source to attend with you.

Entertaining a client can be as simple as going to a movie or taking a walk in the park or at the zoo or around the neighborhood. From my experience, a theater party seems to be a big hit with some people, and I like it, so it kills three birds with one stone—I see a play, I develop a friendship, and I develop a client. (Actually most of my business gifts/ entertainment follow this model.)

Entertaining at home? Women rainmakers' opinions are sharply divided. A Texas rainmaker says, "I entertain people at home—both home cooking and takeout food. I don't do much catering in my home, at least for small dinner parties, but some people do."

But this Illinois rainmaker says, "I never entertain clients in my home. I find myself acting too much like the little housewife, and that's not the image I want to project."

Insist that women be invited to all social/ business-getting functions sponsored by your firm—even sports functions.

A WOMAN partner at an insurance defense firm sponsored a well-publicized alternate outing—a "Day at the Mall" for women adjusters. She arranged transportation to a discount mall and lunch. Supposedly, there was a prize for the person who snagged the best bargains.

IF you sense male clients are uncomfortable with you in a social setting, or if they treat a dinner invitation like a date, invite spouses/significant others to attend. Or try asking a male colleague to attend, or limit social interaction to lunches where business is discussed.

SOME men will still not let a woman pick up a restaurant check. Make it clear when the reservation is made that Ms. So-and-So is the host and she is to get the check. Another way to handle this is to excuse yourself at some point during the meal and advise the maitre d' that the check is to come to you. You can give the maitre d' your credit card in advance, so when the check comes, it has already been put on your card. You need only check the bill for accuracy, add the gratuity, and put your card back in your wallet.

THROW a party! Moving to a new office, a firm anniversary, celebrating a new class of partners, and welcoming an important lateral hire can all be reasons to invite clients and referral sources for refreshment and company. Parties at your own office are relatively inexpensive and remind people who and where you are—even if they must decline the invitation. Set up the buffet in the largest conference room. Use paper and

plastic tableware and bring in platters from a caterer or the grocery store. Make sure desks and offices are neat and no confidential material is lying around. Particularly at holiday time, many law firms will give lavish parties at restaurants or hotel ballrooms. If this is appropriate for your clientele, go for it. But a more modest affair will also be welcome and may better convey your image.

SOMETIMES the best entertaining is accomplished by not going. Give those tickets to the theatre, concert, or ball game to your client or referral source to enjoy with a spouse or child. "Our firm has two season tickets to [fill in the blank]. Would you be interested in a pair on a date convenient to you?" Everyone is busy, and many people put their family time first. In addition, the prospect of being "marketed" may turn off someone who would really appreciate the outing. Give away the tickets, and let them enjoy themselves. While you may not get the opportunity to work on the friendship you were trying to cement, your relationship will benefit from your generosity.

Chapter 9

Inside Your
Law Practice

Rainmakers unanimously agree that everything else you do to market your firm is worthless if the quality of service in your law practice can't live up to the promise of the marketing pitch. No one can guarantee that a client will be able to get everything desired in a negotiation or litigation. What you should be able to guarantee is a stellar level of customer service.

Caring Service

Consider offering free services to get to know your client better. For example, a preventive law checkup may reveal areas of concern of which the client was unaware. This applies to both companies and individuals. Be sure everyone concerned is on board, however. In the "no good deed goes unpunished" category, an attorney who attended condominium board meetings without charge was viewed as snoopy and intrusive by some of the homeowners.

If you want to start a business practice, see what businesses you have some connection to. Say you have some connection to jewelers: find out where their professional association is. Then get a list of the local jewelers, send out something offering to do a business audit of their firm to reveal any exposures they have, and you can start reaching out to them.

G IVEN the choice between presenting a seminar to a group of employees at a business and reviewing files to see the real issues, I'll opt for the business audit/file review every time.

S ET up a Google Alert or electronic clipping service to alert you to mentions of your major clients. If available, subscribe to the RSS Feed from their Website. You can send congratulations when appropriate. But this might also be your first notice of something you need to know about in your work.

I F your state offers a specialty certification program, take advantage of it. Yes, it's a lot of time-consuming effort, but getting that credential will help in all your marketing efforts. You can include the designation reference on your card, stationery, and advertisements. People searching for representation will certainly think more highly of you, and certification will support an appropriate fee.

D ON'T forget ethics. Ethical practice enhances your standing in the community—word does get around. Marketing has its own often highly complex ethical rules. Electronic communications across state lines can trigger multiple states' rules, not all of which may be uniform. Check in with your state bar to make sure you are current on all the requirements, and include disclaimers as appropriate.

Think outside the box to distinguish your practice. Use non-hourly billing (flat fee, reverse contingencies, pure retainer), or unbundle your services (providing limited services for clients who mostly want to go it alone).

O PEN an account with a translation bureau. When a foreign-language-speaking client calls, you will quickly be able to obtain an interpreter with a minimum of fuss.

I MAKE a file to give each new client that has the client's name and matter, my business card, and a pen with our firm name, address, and phone number.

I GARNERED my largest piece of legal business by being courteous to opposing counsel on a legal matter. He remembered me and associated me on a large case when he needed help.

I F your firm does not have an established pro bono program, get one off the ground. If there is one established, make sure you are involved in it. Pro bono work provides young lawyers with training and contacts.

" O FFER a free initial consultation. This is often done through formal channels. I offer free initial consultations on exporting through the Federal Bar Association."

M ANY lawyers, especially those new in practice, are reluctant to send away any potential client. That's a mistake. Trying to tackle an area you know nothing about is one of the classic paths to malpractice. Take only the clients who fit your profile. Send all the others to other lawyers, and let them know the kind of clients you're looking for. Clients will continue to call because you facilitated their business. Plus, the referrals you get back from other lawyers will more than compensate for those you sent away.

Whole Firm Marketing

Be alert to cross-selling opportunities. If you represent small businesses, as part of your full service to your client, you might offer, "Now that you are doing this, do you have your will up-to-date? Do you need a new will? How is your estate planned? If it is a fairly simple matter, I can help you, and if it is fairly complex, I can refer you to an estate specialist."

MAKE sure you network inside as well as outside your firm. Being a rainmaker means creating work for others as well as for yourself. The bigger your firm, the more important is your ability to cross-sell the skills of other lawyers in your firm. Make sure you know all the areas of expertise your firm can offer. Let those lawyers know that you will promote their expertise with your clients. Equally important is for you to communicate to them your strong points and your ability to help other lawyers service their clients. This works for solos and small firms, too, as they build referral networks.

IF you are in a firm with a number of practice areas, identifying opportunities to cross-sell is a very, very important part of marketing. "I'm an environmental lawyer, and if I identify an opportunity for somebody in our real estate section, that lawyer is going to market back to me, so there's marketing that goes on

both inside the firm as well as outside to the community at large. Effective listening is important to be able to identify those opportunities."

THE best way to learn how to do something is to teach it to someone else. Take a more junior lawyer in your firm under your wing, and plan your marketing together.

TAKE a leadership role in your firm. Within your practice area, volunteer to be in charge of marketing.

ASK for marketing help and ideas from others in your firm.

DOES your firm have a marketing coordinator? Resolve to help that person any way you can. The rewards will return tenfold.

BONDING with your firm's professional marketer can help both of you. Many legal marketing professionals are women, and, as non-lawyers, some are in a curious purgatory at the firm. Befriending this person can have many benefits. First, as friends you will naturally share your work experiences. This puts you and your personal practice high on the attention list as something to publicize. The lawyers who neglect to alert the marketing professional to their activities by definition will not get her attention. Second, you can learn marketing techniques from this person, including what parts of your own practice are noteworthy from a marketing standpoint.

USE the guilt factor. Partners want to include women and minorities. Get visible. Confront or suggest to managing partners that women be placed on all the most important committees—*e.g.*, points committee.

INTERNAL firm communications can be just as important to the rainmaker as communication with clients and potential clients. For associates and young partners, you want other rainmakers within your firm to call you to work on their clients' matters. Building relationships with clients is the heart of rainmaking.

Partners should consider how clients are "bequeathed" in their firm. Retiring partners don't always pass clients down to the lawyer who did the most work. Do you project an image of capable management of client relations, besides your competence in your field? Work as hard on rainmaking internally as you do externally for maximum success.

EVEN in the twenty-first century, some firms and clients resist having a woman as lead counsel on a case. If the client is the obstacle, work through a front man who will maintain the primary relationship but give you credit for doing the work. That person should try to educate the client, gently. If movers and shakers in the firm are the obstacle, the best way to demonstrate your ability to first-chair cases is to bring them in and do it.

MARKET as a team, not a solo. Going out on a marketing appointment alone sends a message that your firm is not behind you. This seems particularly true for women. Take at least one other lawyer along for presentations.

Making sure that partners and associates know what you can do goes a long way toward helping you get new clients. Communicating your competence can be a challenge for women in many firms. Women rainmakers report making headway even in the most old-fashioned firms.

Nurturing the Relationship

It takes a whole lot of work to develop a new client, so cherish that relationship. Treat your clients well and provide competent, caring service, and they will refer other clients to you. The value of the referral stream can be many times the worth of an additional single matter, so each client is important, even if they are unlikely to ever have another legal matter for themselves.

Existing clients grow your practice two ways: first, from the additional business they themselves bring, and second, from their referrals. No doubt about it, getting new clients is hard work. Marketing to existing clients is more productive than trolling for new ones.

Have you heard about the 80/20 rule? Eighty percent of your business will come from 20 percent of your clients. Conversely, 80 percent of your headaches will come from (a different) 20 percent of your clients. Cherish the first group, and avoid the latter.

"Work begets work."

Presumably your personality matches your clients' lawyer trait wish list. What do they want? Laid-back and collaborative, or perhaps aggres-

**Deliver more than
you promise.**

sive and rough-edged? Whatever. As long as you perform well utilizing those traits—and they know you're performing well—that is good marketing. Those clients will refer other similarly simpatico clients to you.

MAKE sure the client is confident that you are on the same team. You may not be able to guarantee a result, but you need to stay in tune with your client. An important part of your job is to fully explain the client's options so the client can make informed decisions, such as whether to settle. Never forget that it is the client's case, not yours.

I HAVE found it very helpful to really know my client's business or occupation, even though I am representing them in a family law matter. I have been able to refer customers for their business, so they benefit from knowing me in a way that is not just in the legal arena. Even with people that are not my clients, I try to refer business, and that has helped tremendously. They know I am concerned about their business and therefore look upon me as someone who would work for them in a very positive way.

DON'T ignore other professionals, such as accountants and financial planners, who may also be important referral sources. Those contacts also need to be nurtured.

Chapter 10

Making the Pitch

Are you totally confused by the concept of "making the pitch"? Are you in a quandary about how attorneys can be aggressive marketers while staying within ethical rules? First, understand that the marketer must first get in position to make the pitch. You might meet someone at a networking function and arrange to follow up with a phone call or e-mail. Commonly, you already know the person you're pitching from prior cases, whether representing or opposing this client's interests. You may be following up on an introduction or old school contact. *Everything else you do as a marketer leads up to making a pitch for business.*

Asking for business is one of the hardest things you will ever do—harder than the most difficult case you will ever handle. Feeling comfortable calling on a prospect to make a presentation is a major accomplishment. You can do it.

Research. Research. Research.
Find out as much about your target's business as you can. Check out the target's Website, sure, but also see how that entity is mentioned on other

Websites. Is there a www.PotentialClientSucks.com Website? Not good PR for the target, but maybe a big clue to their legal issues. Check the docket at the courthouse to see if Potential Client is a party, and, if so, to what kind of lawsuits. What has Potential Client's local newspaper been saying lately? When the time is right, diplomatically mention your firm's services that might be helpful.

Be persistent

Churchill was once asked to speak, and the speech that he gave was very, very short. He stood up, and he said, "Never, never, never give up." All of us who are involved in marketing legal services need to adopt the notion that you need to ask, you need to let people know that you want their business. For years, I just thought that people who were my friends will bring me business because they were my friends. That's not true. They needed to know what my business was. They needed to know that I wanted their business. So now I tell people, particularly my friends, what my business is and that I want their business.

How to open the dialogue can be an issue. Standing out from your target's communications tsunami may be difficult, and phone calls may result in unreturned voicemail messages. Sometimes when you finally get through, the person indicates that she is thrilled you did, as she is underwater and lost your prior communications. E-mails may be better, but they can also be lost in the mailbox of an individual who gets two or three hundred a day. Snail mail may be the most effective medium. Besides your classy letterhead, you can send a folder with your firm brochure and other helpful material. The classier the presentation, the more likely it will go on the shelf instead of in the trash. Keep a log of your efforts. It's good to keep trying, but you do have to balance your

efforts against return on investment of time and money. Maybe, indeed, they just don't need you now. Try to stay on the person's radar on at least a sporadic basis so that when she does have that crisis, she knows how to reach you.

Don't be shy

"Let the person know that you are interested in doing their work. I recently realized that although I had been working for a gentleman for more than two years, he was not giving me any new cases. I was taking him to lunch and putting him in contact with other people who could help him in his work, but I saw no new work. Finally, one day I ran into him in the elevator and asked him why he didn't send me any more work. He said, 'You never ask.'"

❝ I DON'T think hungry is a bad way to sound, and I don't think aggressive is necessarily a bad way to sound. After you have done all the preliminary legwork and have created the relationship, and they know who you are and what you do, if you just say, 'Let me know if there is anything I can do for you,' I think you have asked. Sometimes it takes a little bit more than that. For example, you might say, 'Let me know if there is a new case that I can help you out on,' or 'If there is something to do on old case that hasn't closed up the way you would like it to . . . ,' or 'Don't forget that we are here to help you out any-time you need anything.' Those comments are not terribly aggressive. They don't put people on the defensive, and they don't have to respond. You don't want them to feel like they have to explain anything, but you do want them to know you want their work.

"It depends on who I am talking to, but I just ask. I say things like, 'I would really like to have your business,' or 'I would like to help you with new permit problems if you have any of those,' or 'If such-and-such is going to be an issue, let me know if I can be of any help.' To some people I have said, 'Why haven't you sent me any business lately?' I think people are not offended by that; they want to know who wants to do what kind of work.

"I have learned that the premature pitch can be self-defeating. Make the person your friend before you try to make her your client. Pushing too hard makes people push back. Getting pushed away is the last thing you want."

Present Yourself as Plan B

"When asking for new business, here's how to handle the issue of that entity's current representation and if they are happy with it. It depends on who you are talking with and what kind of relationship you have already established with this person. But if this is a non-lawyer and you don't know the person particularly well, I would not be inclined to say, 'I want your business.' I would be inclined to have a more exploratory kind of conversation that starts out with questions like, 'What's going on?' 'What are you working on?' and 'What are you doing?' If legal issues surface in this conversation, ask, 'What are you doing about those? Who is handling that for you? How is it going?' This is a place where you have a lot of learning about this potential client to do, before you are going to be in a position to even know whether it is appropriate to market to them and then to decide how."

WHERE appropriate, approach potential clients who have preexisting legal relationships with competitors. Clients often need backup counsel when conflicts arise.

"WHEN I ask for business, some will say they are already represented in my area by so-and-so. I respond (assuming that I do know something about the firm), 'Yes, that's a very good firm, but if they ever have a conflict, I hope you will keep me in mind.'"

"I AM in a small firm, and sometimes the person who may be referring the business may be dealing with a bigger firm and there may in fact be matters that the big firm can't handle. I met a financial planner and she talked to me first about divorce business. She said to me, 'I send all of my divorce business to so-and-so,' and then she told me about this person's hourly rate, and it was astounding. I said, 'I don't charge nearly that much. He is a wonderful lawyer, and any clients you think are appropriate for him, by all means, send them to him. But if you have clients who could afford more in line with what I charge, I would be very happy to have those clients.'

"I told her my associate does estate planning, and we are very interested in estate planning. She said, 'I send all my estate planning business to so-and-so.' She didn't tell the hourly rate, but she told me who this person was and I knew that that lawyer was in a very large firm. I said, 'Surely, there must be small estate planning matters that firm can't handle.' I told her that we are a very small firm and we are very efficient. We can profitably handle small estate planning matters and are very happy to have them. And now she sends them.

"There are ways to communicate your availability to people who think they already have lawyers, and someday I am going to steal some of that business from some of those big-firm people."

Ask for business

I have always figured that the real goal you are after is to reach that point in a relationship with a client (or non-client) so that you can ask them the prefatory question, 'What do I have to do to get your business?' Have them then lay it out step by step. If you have that relationship (as you will) before you pop the question, they will give you all the prefatory information in bundles that you could possibly need."

"I HAVE to believe there is no such thing as 'No.' There are only different ways to get to 'Yes.' What if you have asked, 'What can I do to get assignments from your company?' and the response is 'Nothing'? Answer: go talk to someone else. If you were approaching the prospect from the top, try wooing the folks at the bottom to create a groundswell. If you were meeting with people at the bottom, try to get a meeting with the people at the top to create a directive."

YOUR best source of new clients is your old clients. Be sure to let clients know the full range of legal needs you can service. Ask clients to refer others who may need services similar to those you've provided to them. If a client compliments you on a job well done, respond by saying, "If you know anyone else who could use our services, please give them my name."

Sometimes a grateful client will say, "Please let me know if there is anything I can do for *you*." Of course, you can say, "We would appreciate your referrals," but you can be more concrete as well. Ask for a recommendation on ***www.LinkedIn.com*** or ***www.Yelp.com***. This will have impact with a much bigger population than just this client's circle of acquaintances.

Mention to other lawyers, "I'd appreciate any work you're conflicted out of."

You never know when an opportunity to make a pitch will arise. "I purchased a car recently, and I asked who handled the dealer's legal work. I ended up representing that car dealership."

To get business, you have to ask. Be enthusiastic about your special interest and practice area. Tell people what you do best and why you do it better. Call or e-mail existing clients to keep in touch, and ask them what other matters they may have. Sell quality rather than price. Asking for referrals ("If you know anyone who needs . . .) is easier than asking for business directly.

If you've been trying to get business from a possible source with no success, come out and ask, "What can we do to get your business?" Maybe there is nothing different you could do. Maybe the prospect won't tell you. But you might learn something important. Perhaps this prospect holds a misconception about your firm. Perhaps the objection is something easily changed. You aren't getting the business anyway, so there's no harm in asking.

Don't be afraid to tell anyone you would like more business.

Don't assume

If you have been working your marketing plan for a number of years, you may have achieved some degree of success and in fact may be perceived

by the outside world as far more successful than you really are. What you may not realize, I think, is that you may be like the most popular girl in high school who doesn't have a date for the prom because all the boys think she already has a date. In other words, there are people out there who might not send you business because they think you are too busy. I have had the experience where lawyers have called me and said that they knew I was so busy because they see my name everywhere, and I know my marketing plan is a success because of this. Then they ask if I could possibly talk to their next-door neighbor about a divorce. I am happy that that happened, but I am wondering about the people who were put off by thinking that I am not available. I think it is very important to communicate to people that you are available. One way to do that is simply by telling them. For example, when people say, "How's it going?" respond, "Business is great, but I am always looking for new clients."

Amazingly, many people assume a lawyer does not want new business. I have had friends say they didn't refer a potential client because they thought I was too busy or didn't need the business. If anyone asks if I'm busy now, I respond, "We're busy, but we can always use more work. That's how we stay busy."

Cross-sell

"Sometimes it feels awkward to promote yourself with a client, but it is very easy to promote the other people in your firm. I can say Susan Young is our environmental expert and I know you have some concerns in this area, so let me put Susan in touch with you because she can help you. It is real easy to promote other people; studies show that clients, by and large, do not know what other services your firm provides. They know what you do, because that is what you are currently working on,

but they often don't know you have these other areas in your firm. That is cross-selling."

PITCH the skills of the male lawyers in your firm to the client who is reluctant to hire a woman. Emphasize that the client will have available the full resources of your organization.

SUGGEST to clients other areas where you can be of help. This opportunity often arises in litigation. Litigators may find an area where the client is facing potential legal problems—badly drafted contracts, employee policies, etc. Bring them to the client's attention, suggest a remedy, and offer your firm's services.

Meet the Prospect

Don't be afraid to get on a plane to travel to make your pitch. Putting the face with the voice is an important part of building rapport. Webcams and videoconferencing can help, but it's still not the same as being able to press the flesh. Many clients (or potential clients) will try to dissuade you from traveling just to see them. Apparently, they don't want to feel beholden that you have incurred these expenses solely for their benefit. Find a reason to travel to the area—a professional meeting or seminar, perhaps? Maybe it's seeing someone else—"I have to be in your area to visit another client." Once you have the first appointment confirmed, if you are disclosing client names (or hints of names), you can bootstrap to the other appointments. A drawback to asking to visit on a specific day is if the person you want to see has a conflict. Get around this by starting the conversation like this: "I have to be in your area 'next week' or 'in [pick a month],' but I can be flexible. What would be a good day to come visit with you?"

" **I** ONCE took a general counsel to lunch to ask for business. We had previously been on opposite sides of a case, so we knew each other pretty well. Some men are uncomfortable with a woman picking up the check, and he tried to pay for the lunches. I told him, 'Oh no, *I* am the one hustling *you*.'"

FOLLOW up a compliment on your work with a request for more. "We were very impressed with your efforts," is nice. A good response is, "Thank you. I look forward to working with you on your California cases in the future."

" **I** WAS representing a paper company, and, as it turned out, they were part of a big conglomerate, and actually the legal work was assigned out of New York. But I had to ask at the local office where I was already representing them, 'How do I get more business?'"

IF you are lucky enough to be asked to respond to a request for proposal, make sure your response exactly matches the stated requirements. Women do seem to be more meticulous about these kinds of things. Overlooking one of the questions can kill your prospects in the first round.

YOU'VE made the contact with a potential client. What do you do now to raise yourself from the level of "acceptable" to "most desirable counsel"?

Let's assume you've already learned the general nature of the company's legal service needs. It's time to get specific. What did

the client like most and least about prior outside counsel? How is your own experience and expertise superior in substance and/or delivery? Be prepared to articulate why you are uniquely qualified to meet this potential client's needs.

State exactly the nature of work you are prepared to accept and what you do not handle (and why). Nothing impresses less than the appearance of wanting any kind of work at all. Selectivity confers credibility.

Be prepared to specify the following:

- What cases have you handled that relate to the needs you would like to serve?
- What training, seminars, CLE programs, etc. have you experienced that uniquely qualify you?
- What technology, support staff, equipment, etc. do you have to help you meet deadlines and achieve the quality you promise?
- What preparation have you undertaken for doing this work—*e.g.*, research, reading?
- What unique—even creative—ideas do you have for this client's work?

Schedule your meeting during regular business hours at the client's office. When scheduling your meeting, be specific about its purpose and length. An hour is more than enough, although forty-five minutes is less intrusive and will demonstrate your superior organization! Enhance the probability of getting the appointment by suggesting alternate times from which the prospective client can choose.

In the meeting, get to the point early. Explain your analysis of what the client and the client's support team seem to need and want, and identify what they've been getting and wish they hadn't been getting. Explain your process and conclusions. Be very, very specific. Then, seek feedback. Find out how they feel about your presentation. Ask for candor.

You're not finished until you have a commitment from the client to send you work. Failing a commitment, see if you can ascertain what else you need to do to earn work. If there is no match for you, determine what types of matters she does think you are well suited for and she is comfortable referring.

These recommendations assume your basic communication skills and sound judgment.

Afterword

You're a baseball player now. After reading this book, you not only know how to position yourself to market (the windup), but you are ready to ask for business (make the pitch). No matter the size of your team, you need to ensure your own marketing excellence to enhance your position on that team or make you an attractive acquisition for other teams.

A planned marketing program is neither simple nor easy. It requires time. Marketing is intuitive to some; others study and approach the task with structured method. Wherever your own marketing skills fall on the spectrum, hopefully this book has provided new ideas and will stimulate you to create even more ideas for your unique practice.

As you and your practice mature, your marketing will change to fit your personal and professional goals. Each time you pick up this book, your ideas will be different. Your new perspective will produce fresh ideas. Thank you for letting this book be the catalyst.

About the Author

Theda (Teddy) Snyder has practiced in firms of varying sizes, as a solo and as in-house counsel. She is currently with Ringler Associates, a national structured settlement brokerage, in the Beverly Hills, California, office.

Ms. Snyder is the author of two prior editions of *Women Rainmakers' Best Marketing Tips* as well as *Running a Law Practice on a Shoestring*, all published by the American Bar Association Law Practice Management Section. She has also written numerous published articles and spoken to many trade and legal groups.

In 1990, Ms. Snyder was among a group of women attorneys who put together the first Women Rainmakers American Bar Association annual meeting program. That committee evolved into the Women Rainmakers Interest Group within the Law Practice Management Section. Ms. Snyder was a founding co-chair.

Index

INDEX

INDEX

INDEX

Selected Books from . . .
THE ABA LAW PRACTICE MANAGEMENT SECTION

The Lawyer's Guide to Collaboration Tools and Technologies: Smart Ways to Work Together
By Dennis Kennedy and Tom Mighell
This first-of-its-kind guide for the legal profession shows you how to use standard technology you already have and the latest "Web 2.0" resources and other tech tools, like Google Docs, Microsoft Office and Share-Point, and Adobe Acrobat, to work more effectively on projects with colleagues, clients, co-counsel and even opposing counsel. In *The Lawyer's Guide to Collaboration Tools and Technologies: Smart Ways to Work Together*, well-known legal technology authorities Dennis Kennedy and Tom Mighell provides a wealth of information useful to lawyers who are just beginning to try these tools, as well as tips and techniques for those lawyers with intermediate and advanced collaboration experience.

The Lawyer's Guide to Marketing on the Internet, Third Edition
By Gregory H. Siskind, Deborah McMurray, and Richard P. Klau
In today's competitive environment, it is critical to have a comprehensive online marketing strategy that uses all the tools possible to differentiate your firm and gain new clients. The Lawyer's Guide to Marketing on the Internet, in a completely updated and revised third edition, showcases practical online strategies and the latest innovations so that you can immediately participate in decisions about your firm's Web marketing effort. With advice that can be implemented by established and young practices alike, this comprehensive guide will be a crucial component to streamlining your marketing efforts.

The 2010 Solo and Small Firm Legal Technology Guide
By Sharon D. Nelson, Esq., John W. Simek, and Michael C. Maschke
This annual guide is the only one of its kind written to help solo and small firm lawyers find the best technology for their dollar. You'll find the most current information and recommendations on computers, servers, networking equipment, legal software, printers, security products, smart phones, and anything else a law office might need. It's written in clear, easily understandable language to make implementation easier if you choose to do it yourself, or you can use it in conjunction with your IT consultant. Either way, you'll learn how to make technology work for you.

The Lawyer's Guide to Adobe Acrobat, Third Edition
By David L. Masters
This book was written to help lawyers increase productivity, decrease costs, and improve client services by moving from paper-based files to digital records. This updated and revised edition focuses on the ways lawyers can benefit from using the most current software, Adobe® Acrobat 8, to create Portable Document Format (PDF) files.

PDF files are reliable, easy-to-use, electronic files for sharing, reviewing, filing, and archiving documents across diverse applications, business processes, and platforms. The format is so reliable that the federal courts' Case Management/Electronic Case Files (CM/ECF) program and state courts that use Lexis-Nexis File & Serve have settled on PDF as the standard.

You'll learn how to:
- Create PDF files from a number of programs, including Microsoft Office
- Use PDF files the smart way
- Markup text and add comments
- Digitally, and securely, sign documents
- Extract content from PDF files
- Create electronic briefs and forms

The Law Firm Associate's Guide to Personal Marketing and Selling Skills
By Catherine Alman MacDonagh and Beth Marie Cuzzone
This is the first volume in ABA's new groundbreaking Law Firm Associates Development Series, created to teach important skills that associates and other lawyers need to succeed at their firms, but that they may have not learned in law school. This volume focuses on personal marketing and sales skills. It covers creating a personal marketing plan, finding people within your target market, preparing for client meetings, "asking" for business, realizing marketing opportunities, keeping your clients, staying in touch with your network inside and outside the firm, and more. An accompanying trainer's manual illustrating how to best structure the sessions and use the book is available to firms to facilitate group training sessions.

Many law firms expect their new associates to hit the ground running when they are hired on. Although firms often take the time to bring these associates up to speed on client matters, they can be reluctant to invest the time needed to train them how to improve personal skills such as marketing. This book will serve as a brief, easy-to-digest primer for associates on how to develop and use marketing and selling techniques.

ABA **LawPracticeManagementSection**
MARKETING • MANAGEMENT • TECHNOLOGY • FINANCE

The Lawyer's Guide to Microsoft Word 2007
By Ben M. Schorr

Microsoft Word is one of the most used applications in the Microsoft Office suite—there are few applications more fundamental than putting words on paper. Most lawyers use Word and few of them get everything they can from it. Because the documents you create are complex and important—your law practice depends, to some degree, upon the quality of the documents you produce and the efficiency with which you can produce them. Focusing on the tools and features that are essential for lawyers in their everyday practice, *The Lawyer's Guide to Microsoft Word* explains in detail the key components to help make you more effective, more efficient and more successful.

Introduction to Law Firm Practice
By Michael Downey

Navigating your way through a law firm practice can be overwhelming, especially in larger firms. A firm is made up of equity and non-equity partners, senior attorneys, senior associates, "Of Counsel" designates, associates, and interns, in addition to the paralegals, managers, and support staff that all help make a law firm run effectively and efficiently. A new guide by the ABA Law Practice Management Section, *Introduction to Law Firm Practice*, is a systematic study of how lawyers practice law at private firms and will help you navigate your way through how a law firm operates.

Find Info Like a Pro, Volume 1: Mining the Internet's Publicly Available Resources for Investigative Research
By Carole A. Levitt and Mark E. Rosch

This complete hands-on guide shares the secrets, shortcuts, and realities of conducting investigative and background research using the sources of publicly available information available on the Internet. Written for legal professionals, this comprehensive desk book lists, categorizes, and describes hundreds of free and fee-based Internet sites. The resources and techniques in this book are useful for investigations; depositions; locating missing witnesses, clients, or heirs; and trial preparation, among other research challenges facing legal professionals. In addition, a CD-ROM is included, which features clickable links to all of the sites contained in the book.

Social Media for Lawyers
By Carolyn Elefant and Nicole Black

The world of legal marketing has changed with the rise of social media sites such as Linkedin, Twitter, and Facebook. Law firms are seeking their companies attention with tweets, videos, blog posts, pictures, and online content. Social media is fast and delivers news at record pace. Social Media for Lawyers: The Next Frontier provides you with a practical, goal-centric approach to using social media in your law practice that will enable you to identify social media platforms and tools that fit your practice and implement them easily, efficiently, and ethically.

30-Day Risk-Free Order Form
Call Today! 1-800-285-2221
Monday–Friday, 7:30 AM – 5:30 PM, Central Time

Qty	Title	LPM Price	Regular Price	Total
_____	The Lawyer's Guide to Collaboration Tools and Technologies:			
	Smart Ways to Work Together (5110589)	$59.95	$ 89.95	$_____
_____	The Lawyer's Guide to Marketing on the Internet, Third Edition (5110585)	74.95	84.95	$_____
_____	The 2010 Solo and Small Firm Legal Technology Guide (5110701)	54.95	89.95	$_____
_____	The Lawyer's Guide to Adobe Acrobat, Third Edition (5110588)	49.95	79.95	$_____
_____	The Law Firm Associate's Guide to Personal Marketing and Selling Skills (5110582)	39.95	49.95	$_____
_____	The Lawyer's Guide to Microsoft Word 2007 (5110697)	49.95	69.95	$_____
_____	Introduction to Law Firm Practice (5110703)	47.95	79.95	$_____
_____	Find Info Like a Pro, Volume 1: Mining the Internet's Publicly Available			
	Resources for Investigative Research (5110708)	47.95	79.95	$_____
_____	Social Media for Lawyers (5110710)	47.95	79.95	$_____

*Postage and Handling	
$10.00 to $49.99	$5.95
$50.00 to $99.99	$7.95
$100.00 to $199.99	$9.95
$200.00+	$12.95

**Tax	
DC residents add 5.75%	
IL residents add 10.25%	

*Postage and Handling	$_____
**Tax	$_____
TOTAL	$_____

PAYMENT

❏ Check enclosed (to the ABA)   Name

❏ Visa   ❏ MasterCard   ❏ American Express

_____   _____   _____
Account Number   Exp. Date   Signature

Firm _____

Address _____

City _____   State _____   Zip _____

Phone Number _____   E-Mail Address _____

Guarantee
If—for any reason—you are not satisfied with your purchase, you may
return it within 30 days of receipt for a complete refund of the price of the
book(s). No questions asked!

Mail: ABA Publication Orders, P.O. Box 10892, Chicago, Illinois 60610-0892
♦ Phone: 1-800-285-2221 ♦ FAX: 312-988-5568

E-Mail: abasvcctr@abanet.org ♦ Internet: http://www.lawpractice.org/catalog